FROM SQUEAK TO ROAR

Unleashing the Potential in your

Relationship Marketing Tribe

SECOND EDITION

Angelyn Toth

Testimonial

Angelyn Toth most certainly accomplishes her stated goal of being an ambassador for the industry of Relationship Marketing and she does so with deep insight born of long experience and unarguable success at the trade. The analogies of animal behaviors with those of business team members are delivered with specificity and compelling logic that illuminate and entertain all at once. Each of her animals paints the picture of a surprisingly recognizable human being, with whom any reader will be familiar in some degree. Her invitation to her readers to look for their own traits among her descriptions, lends a hands-on/how-to aspect that offers a practical way of understanding and adjusting behaviors that may be undermining business success.

What is most unique, refreshing and inspirational about it all, is Angelyn's clearly genuine passion and contagious joy for the industry in which she has been so successful and for which she offers her readers a path to similar accomplishment.

It's a very, very rare thing to hear a business figure speak movingly of heart and service to humanity and it is this humane and greatly likable perspective that gives her voice such credibility and appeal and sells the idea of her industry being one worth entering.

Rhonda, Editor

Amazing work!!! (Continued from back cover:)

It's smart, playful and insightful all at once. You will instantly recognize the personality and behaviors of team members you know in each of her animals and as a result you will be able to better help yourself and your team breakthrough the limiting patterns that may be sabotaging your success.

Angelyn is uniquely qualified to lead you to success. This is your heart to heart conversation with someone that not only did it, but has and is still helping so many others to do the same. Angelyn shares the secrets of what it takes to reach the top of the Relationship Marketing Industry. From beginning to end, she offers valuable insights from her unmatched experience in the industry, taking you step by step through not only the "How To" of MLM, but she also shares the personal development changes you must make to become ultimately successful. One of the most delightful aspects of the book is Angelyn's joyful, optimistic, energy which shines throughout — this, in itself, is a clear demonstration of the mindset necessary for success in life.

This great book is a must-read for new distributors, seasoned network marketing leaders, and corporate staff alike.

Dave O'Connor is an International Keynote Speaker and Mindset Expert to Top Network Marketing Companies. www.daveoconnoronline.com

This book is a MUST READ for it bridges the understanding of the variety in the animal world with the differences in human beings to deepen our appreciation for diversity. If you are looking to improve your ability to communicate effectively with others, as well as with yourself, this book provides insight and action steps for positive outcomes. If you are building a team, this book will provide the context for transformative growth, and may even reduce the growing pains! Angelyn's wisdom comes through with real stories that drive home the key messages that would be spoken by our animal friends if they could speak for themselves.

Renee Poindexter, Living the Potential Network. Principal Facilitator "Bring all of who you are to everything you do!"

Illustrated by Jessie Flynn

ISBN

978-1-4602-7947-2 (Hardcover)

978-1-4602-7038-7 (Paperback)

978-1-4602-7948-9 (eBook)

Produced by:

FriesenPress

Suite 300 – 990 Fort Street

Victoria, BC, Canada V8V 3K2

www.friesenpress.com

Distributed to the trade by The Ingram Book Company

Table of Contents

Dedication vii

Acknowledgements viii

Introduction x

Chapter 1 3
What or Who Makes up Your Tribe?

Chapter 2 7
Beaver — *Dream Builder*

Chapter 3 11
Care Bear — *Caregiver*

Chapter 4 15
Cats — *Entitled*

Chapter 5 21
Deer — *Innocent*

Chapter 6 27
Dog — *Loyal*

Chapter 7 31
Dolphin — *Enthusiastic*

Chapter 8 35
Eagle — *Visionary Leader*

Chapter 9 39
Hare — *Erratic*

Chapter 10 45
Horse — *Born to Run*

Chapter 11 51
Lone Wolf — *Elusive*

Chapter 12 57
Lynx — *Seer*

Chapter 13 63
Mouse — *Plays a Small Game*

Chapter 14 75
Peacock — *Rock Star or Diva*

Chapter 15 81
Shark — *Caution*

Chapter 16 85
Sheep — *Sheepish*

Chapter 17 89
  Skunk — *Reputation*
Chapter 18 95
  Tortoise — *Our Customers*
Chapter 19 97
  Summarizing Part One
Chapter 20 102
  Issues that Hold People Back
Chapter 21 109
  How to Warm Up a Cold Market
Chapter 22 117
  Journey from Willingness to Readiness
Chapter 23 128
  Template for Success
Chapter 24 133
  Expectations and Perceptions
Chapter 25 136
  Volunteer Leadership
Chapter 26 142
  **More Great Reasons to Take this
  Path of Relationship Marketing**
Chapter 27 151
  It Really Is Important to Do Your Thing
Chapter 28 158
  **Old School Thought vs. New School Thought about
  Relationship Marketing**
Chapter 29 164
  **Important Things to Know About this Profession of
  Relationship Marketing**
Chapter 30 168
  The Potential of Socially Responsible Businesses
Chapter 31 172
  Being in Love with this Business
Chapter 32 176
  A Connecting Force
About the Author 180
About the Illustrator 183

Dedication

I dedicate this book to the most precious relationship of my lifetime and that is with my beloved daughter Kasara Toth. Her very presence in my life has blessed me with knowing and experiencing unconditional love.

I also dedicate it to you, the one holding this book. Thank you for having the courage to go for your dreams.

Acknowledgements

I have to begin by acknowledging my Relationship Marketing Tribe and Mentors. I have learned so much from every one of you and feel a deep gratitude. I cannot mention every one of you by name because it would take pages and pages but you know who you are. Some I will mention are: Wendy Sobieski, Harry Mathers, Ariel Cantin, Sara Spicer, Dr.Neil Tessler, Andrea Huber, Carol Walters, Tina Colter, Mellen Mathers, Rheja Gilchrist, Dr.Arlette Alexander, Julie Blue, Marina Richards, Loretta James, Marilyn Foreman, France Laberge and the Campbell River team, David Kleber and Rhetah Kwan, Bob and Renate Lundberg, Ralph Beitz, Stephen Cherniske, Natalie Kather, Al and Jan Keranen, Ron and Jan Boyanovsky, Michael Oliver, Dave O'Connor and Carla Rieger. Special thanks to Eric Worre and his great book: Go Pro. He has had a big impact in transforming Network Marketing to its well-deserved professional status.

This book would not have even been possible if it weren't for Renee Poindexter. She brought me into her Tribe and together we expanded to include many more members. She is one of the most devoted people I know and a great visionary and leader.

Bill Lee — I want to thank the most generous, visionary owner and Chairman of a truly great Relationship Marketing Company.

Elinor Meney — My wonderful Instinx Coach and friend. Thank you Elinor for your constant support in helping me through the many levels of this journey

Diane Leclair — Diane gifted me 100 hours of her time in contribution to getting my book out. Thanks for being a catalyst and cheerleader.

Chrystalle Grace — My best friend and greatest supporter, who passed away in October 2010 before seeing my book published. But I know she is aware and still cheering me on.

Saria Cundall — An angel, who came into my life at the perfect time. She manages my retreat centre Xenia and supports me *over the top*.

Dale Hamilton — A soul brother, who has supported Xenia and me in extraordinary ways. I cannot wait to see his book coming out very soon.

Lucas Gaudette — Our fantastic web designer (www.xeniacentre. com and angelyntoth.com). Thanks for your support with book title, web sites and much more.

Thanks to my special "readers," Christina Toth, Renee Poindexter, and Tina Overbury.

Jessie Flynn — My Illustrator. Wow Jessie you are an amazing artist. I love your talent and am so grateful you collaborated with me on this book. From the first time I met Jessie many years ago we had an instant bond and I consider her an adopted daughter. Thanks for sharing your gift with the world.

Last but not least — Kasara Toth, my amazing daughter who supported me so much to do this book. Not only encouraging me, she took the time, while at school doing her doctorate degree, to painstakingly go over and over my manuscript and help shape it into something legible and enjoyable to read. She is an awesome teacher and her courage and fortitude to become a veterinarian has inspired me to go for my dreams.

Introduction

By your picking up this book, we have already passed first base. Either you don't know anything about Relationship Marketing and have likely never been exposed to it; or you have had a pleasant experience with it and want to find out more. Perhaps you were intrigued by the title of the book or by the animal images you noticed while flipping through the book. There might be the odd case where it dropped off the shelf into your arms. Anyway, for whatever reason, *From Squeak to Roar* is open in your hands right now, I would like to welcome you to a way of doing business where you can not only succeed but you can also have an impact.

First I'd like to tell you a little bit about how I got involved in the business of Relationship Marketing and to explain exactly what it is. Then I'd like to ask you a few questions.

My Journey with Relationship Marketing

I have been involved in Relationship Marketing for ten short years. During this time, I have been radically changed by the experience. I won the Associate of the Year Award for North America in 2008 for exemplary leadership, the Rock Star Award in 2010, a BMW car allowance for the past six years and was inducted into the Millionaire Club in 2013. I have served on the Advisory Board with the company corporate team for several years. This year I was the recipient of the most prestigious 2015 Award given by my company for servant leadership and loyalty and excellence in character. And I am still an active participant and leader in the same company.

When this Relationship Marketing opportunity was offered to me back in 2005, my mind said, *absolutely no way. Never.* I literally said *no* six times to my friend when she approached me. I didn't like the idea and I had heard many a bad tale about the industry so I wanted nothing to do with it. However, I was in dire straights financially and had a large thirty-eight-acre retreat centre to support and a daughter on her way to vet school. Did I have a need? Yes. But was I interested? No.

Being the astute person my friend is, she offered me some products that she thought could help with my injured knee and the fatigue I was feeling. Fortunately for me and for her, that's exactly what happened. I had an excellent product experience pretty quickly and was on-board to buy some products right away. As for joining her in the business, I was still not interested.

I really didn't believe it was possible to earn significant money and I questioned the ethics of such a system. I had an old paradigm viewpoint and wrong information about the process and nearly didn't recognize it as the miracle I had been praying for. Patiently my friend educated me as to what Relationship Marketing is today. Thank God for her tenacity and my need aligning at the perfect time. There was a divine plan that was greater than my resistance and I jumped on board wholeheartedly and never looked back.

So you can imagine how earning my first million dollars in Relationship Marketing was a mind-blowing surprise, considering the intense battle I had waged before getting on board. Going from near bankruptcy to Millionaire Club is an astonishing change of trajectory. My retreat centre is now in its twenty second year and my daughter has completed her doctorate degree at the Western College of Veterinary Medicine. We are grateful beyond belief.

The thing that has kept me engaged, though, is not the money, cars, trips, or recognition but more the opportunity to live my life on purpose, with values intact. All the wealth doesn't compare to the joy of making a difference in other people's lives. To me, that is what is fulfilling and rewarding; to see others fulfill their dreams and grow in ways I had never witnessed before in the corporate world. Nothing compares to seeing my team blossom; to supporting individuals who were once sick, stuck and unhappy, who have transformed before my very eyes.

What is Relationship Marketing? (Also referred to as Network Marketing).

In a nutshell, it is a professional entrepreneurial system with a residual income where everyone has as much to gain. It is a co-operative style and win/win process, which makes it totally unique. It's not so much about selling products as it is about marketing, education and big picture. It's more about people helping people because you can only succeed in this Profession if you help others to succeed. What a brilliant and conscious business model. I call it a "fair and elegant way to win." It is a profession gaining great respect, applications for today's economy, and vast technological capabilities. It is a word-of-mouth, referral-based business with a low cost of entry and unlimited potential. We are in Relationship Marketing together, to support each other's dreams and talents as we create our own inclusive economy and foster customer loyalty. An associate or distributor takes on a role as educator or consultant and the company pays you for this referral and training service.

Now for the questions:

If, in this book, you could find a way of perceiving people in Relationship Marketing in a new light, would you be interested? If you could start to understand what encourages and inspires your team, would this be useful? If you could understand the different characteristics and stages you and your team will go through in order to succeed, would you want to know?

Great. I'm assuming your answer is yes since you are continuing to read on.

From Squeak to Roar was conceived out of another book I was writing, one I had started four years earlier called: Invisible Rules of the Game. In a way, it was as if my book had a baby and that baby became more urgent and demanded more of my attention. So Invisible Rules of the Game took a back seat while From Squeak to Roar poured out of me in a curious way. Most times I would be hiking with my dog when this book started knocking at my door. Ideas, concepts and images flooded my mind while I puffed my way up the very steep incline. The first time it happened, I grabbed my iPhone and spoke the words that were tumbling out, into the recorder.

Amused by the journey, I opened myself up to the process and sure enough, it started to happen daily as my dog and I hiked up to our favourite lake. One day, I was thinking about sheep when suddenly an eagle called right above my head and insisted on my attention. So I moved from logical thinking mind (my will), to the universal-big-picture-mind of (Thy will). Inspiration and intuitive intelligence took over. It happened over and over again as different animals started revealing themselves to me. Sometimes I would catch myself chuckling at the insights each animal brought and how they correlated with a particular person on my team. I loved the process — it appealed to the kid in me. I hope it does for you too.

There was a time when this unexpected inspiration didn't happen and I missed its presence but I always trusted the timing and what was being shown to me. Just when I thought for sure I had all of the animals (fifteen of them), two more showed up. They were Deer and Lynx. Deer seemed obvious since I am literally surrounded by them at the retreat centre where I live. What's more, once I got the message, I started to find them in my team as clear as day. Last but not least, Lynx showed up — in character, I may add; meaning in a very mysterious way.

Life speaks to us in messages and clues, if we pay attention. It is not mysterious; it is actually quite normal. I must admit it can be difficult to tune in when you are so busy living life, going to work, commuting, taking care of the kids etc. When you tune in, you too will start noticing how life is always offering support and guidance. I'm not going to get religious but some would say it is Divine presence speaking to us.

Living in a rain forest on a small island with thirty-eight acres of woods and meadows, I have a definite advantage in tuning-in to the abundance of nature. We have horses, a potbelly pig, a dog, and a cat and they are all unique characters. I live on the edge of a bird sanctuary, sandwiched between two lakes; a fifteen-minute walk to the ocean. There is such a harmony I feel in nature and whenever I am stressed out — I step outside and within minutes I am renewed. This creative process happens more when I am tuned-in to nature. There have been many times where I was struggling over a speech or presentation I had to give. The moment I stepped outside and began walking, the ideas came tumbling into my consciousness. I remember once an entire plan for a workshop came to me…in order. It was like taking dictation. I had to keep stopping to jot down notes but what a great way to get the job done.

This book combines the knowledge gleaned by living and succeeding in the world of relationship marketing for the past eight years. It is also informed by my passion for and lifetime of experience with animals. I gathered these insights while painstakingly trying to understand how this industry of Relationship Marketing works — and how it is different. I have used my familiarity with members of my team and people I have seen in other companies to create the material and you may find yourself in one or more of the animals. Don't worry; I won't call you out by name. Remember these are stages and phases rather than who you are. You will learn ways to transform when you are ready. The most important thing is to be easy on yourself as you stretch to higher ground. This is the secret. This is the power.

You will notice that *From Squeak to Roar* doesn't include a Lion but it points to moving from a timid voice to an empowered state. This book is about helping you find your Roar.

My wish for you is to enjoy this book and discover the subtleties and secrets of mastering your Relationship Marketing business. Share it with your teams and discover the unspoken truth between the words. There you will find me.

Relationship Marketing is not for the faint of heart but for those who are ready - it is the ride of a lifetime.
Angelyn

PART ONE —
Who is Showing up in Your Tribe?

Chapter 1

What or Who Makes up Your Tribe?

Let's begin with — What is a Tribe?

It is a group of distinct members, coming together over a shared vision with a common culture. You may be a member of a couple of different Tribes and you may come and go with your presence. A Tribe is not about a specific place or event, it's more of a feeling, or resonance. It's like a soul family with a belonging atmosphere.

In Relationship Marketing you are likely to have thousands of people in your business. Some of them will be part of the Tribe experience and many may not — even though they are in your team. The ones who make up the infrastructure of your Tribe are likely the members who are connected and contributing. Your Tribe is not like the in-crowd. It's not based on inclusivity or exclusivity but is more of a volunteer brand — an opting-in, if you will. Resonance is the main feature. Forming a Tribe is not even something you have to set out to do but instead you need only be open to the potential of like-minded and like-hearted people joining your endeavour.

So what defines the Tribe?

- The Resonance
- The Culture
- The Need
- The Contribution

Our core values create the resonance. There will be many different types of Tribes, all resonating because of shared core values. Not right or wrong, not better or worse but connected by a common thread of perfect alignment.

From Squeak to Roar is about the unique compilation of individuals that you attract to your Tribe and about understanding the dynamics we create together. It is based on the whole gamut of personalities; from timid to audacious and everything in-between. Through the knowledge of these dynamics, you will learn how to lead and influence with integrity.

As we embark on this journey together, we will bring awareness to the ways in which we contribute to building a loyal and successful team. The people on your team will inevitably come from a variety of backgrounds, professions, and experiences; each having a unique style and different reasons for his or her attraction to Relationship Marketing.

By sharing this book, my biggest hope is to open pathways of awareness about this Profession and the huge benefits it brings when you step forward with real communication and connection. I'm not going to tell you that you will get rich quick or that your entire life will transform by reading these words. Though, come to think of it, it may. Instead, I invite you to study the content of *From Squeak to Roar*. Play with it and see what happens when you bring the book's purpose of understanding and support to your teams.

I have selected seventeen different animals to depict the characteristics and stages we may go through. I chose animals as a symbol of these stages as it provides a universal, yet familiar way of understanding the concepts I will be presenting. I see this business as a wonderful game, and it seemed fun to use animal symbolism. The game is real however; it is a game with real results that change lives.

As you explore the following animal categories, you may find places where you or your team may be stuck. The intention is to allow us to look at ways in which we can transform ourselves and move forward. That being said, I want to be clear how important it is to trust and accept that not everyone in our business is on a "growth path." We have to support our team members wherever they are and perhaps further support those who are genuinely drawn to this path of Self-Actualization. Oops.... maybe I let the cat out of the bag too soon but really, this business model is a personal and professional development program with a compensation plan. Every step you take towards success will offer plenty of opportunities for growth, that is, if you decide to take up the challenge. And if you do, I can assure you, you will be embarking upon a process of transformation. There is a direct parallel between your level of success and your personal development, no matter what area of industry you are involved in. I love what Jim Rohn once said: *"Work on your job and you will make a living. Work on your Self and you will make a fortune."*[1]

I suggest you do not tell people what animals they are but let them discover the qualities for themselves. You will be surprised how people perceive themselves and how different their perceptions may be to how you view them. Since perception influences reality, their perception is what counts.

I have attempted to bring the invisible into the visible by my observations and direct experience.

Of course I had to walk this journey first over the past eight years and I offer this humbly to you as my gift.

The seventeen animals are not judged by priority or as a hierarchy and so I have placed them in alphabetical order.

---

1   Rohn, Jim. *The Art of Exceptional Living.* Nightingale-Conant; (1993) Audio

Chapter 2

Beaver — *Dream Builder*

Consider yourself really lucky if you have a Beaver or two in your business. They have an aptitude to hold and carry out a big vision. They are diligent, productive, do whatever it takes to get the job done and do not keep score. (Well, they try not to.) They have an incredible work ethic; forging their way towards a large team with you. They are great engineers, navigate systems well, and are very resourceful. Beavers' level of commitment is solid and they have the capacity to carry out extraordinary tasks. They are great team players and go over the top with everyone who joins their team. Beavers multi-task because there is always so much to do. They never question the work that has to be done. Beavers have an undeniable fortitude and are never concerned about going the distance.

Although they say they don't need acknowledgment, they do love recognition for a job well done. This witnessing helps them to be their highest and best. And whether we admit it or not, we all love being seen and acknowledged.

Sometimes Beavers are so busy *doing* that they forget to relax and let others take up the slack. In a way, they feel they have to fill in for everyone. When they're out of balance, they tend to be a little whiney and sacrifice themselves, which is never a good thing.

Keeping stride with Beavers can be daunting at times because they have such a big capacity to get the job done. Rather than compare yourself with them, see if you can learn some gems from them. Maybe your way is different and you could be just as effective, so watch out that you stay true to yourself.

Beavers do not get knocked off their course easily and if they do momentarily, they will be back in the game very quickly.

<u>What you can learn from Beavers:</u>

- A healthy work ethic.
- Commitment
- Loyalty and honour
- What passion for a vision looks and operates like.
- Expertise in building a strong infrastructure.
- Resourcefulness

<u>How to enthuse Beavers:</u>

- Don't take advantage of their addiction to working so hard.
- Pick up the slack and join forces with them.
- Offer gratitude and kindness.
- Lead, follow, or get out of their way.

<u>If you are at the Beaver stage, transformation is possible if:</u>

- You learn how to say "NO."
- You notice that if resentment is creeping in, you are overdoing it.
- When you are uptight and stressed out, you can relax and ask for help.
- You better BALANCE your life — otherwise burnout could happen.
- You remember to have FUN because you are a role model and your team is watching you.
- You let the game come to you a little more, instead of pushing so hard.

- You are willing to trust in the resources available to you.
- You hold others accountable, instead of doing it all yourself.
- You watch out for the tendency to be a martyr and being all things to all people.
- You TRUST others more.

I have had the privilege of partnering with some amazing Beavers and love and respect them tremendously. What I notice is when you are passionate about what you do, you may appear to others as a workaholic but really it is because you have a big capacity and strong drive. I truly believe that to pull off a big vision, you have to be a bit of a workaholic but when it is your passion, it doesn't feel like work. It is simply something you have to do.

Sometimes though, I have to remind the Beavers that it's important to model balance. After all, Relationship Marketing is a business about health, wealth, purpose and time freedom.

Chapter 3

Care Bear — *Caregiver*

Care Bears are sincere, authentic caregivers, who play an important role in this business. They may not be fast but they are loving and persistent and they bring great support to your team. When they move up the levels — their success brings joy to everyone involved. They usually default there because of attracting some great people to their teams...It's not that they are not great business people but they truly are not keeping score and watching numbers at the end of the month. You will find them taking care of the registration table, because they are happiest in a support role.

They particularly love the *pay it forward* concept of this business and for this alone, they will join your community.

Even though it is their natural state of being, Care Bears do have a tendency to overdo the care of others. They have a pattern of wanting to save and help people in need and can be a little self-sacrificing. Operating from a pattern of saving others is usually not effective and can create a sense of failure for all involved. Care Bears may not recognize that in the bigger picture, it would be better to attract people who are capable and less needy. By not doing so, they are holding themselves back. It's a fine line between supporting and enabling, and Care Bears have to watch out for this line. Having said that — success can be measured in so many different ways, and for Care Bears, success is really helping others to succeed. And if it's done right with a little strategy thrown in, they too can succeed financially — especially when other members of the Tribe return the favour and bring their gifts to substitute for the weaknesses in Care Bears. Together we have it all.

<u>What you can learn from Care Bears:</u>

- How to be unconditional in your support for others.
- How service is the cornucopia of this business.
- The importance of more intrinsic goals.
- What patience and kindness looks and feels like.

<u>How to enthuse your Care Bears:</u>

- Love and support them as they do so willingly for others.
- Give them acknowledgment for their contributions.
- Offer them forward-moving action steps towards their dreams.
- Be willing to be their coach and listen to them CAREfully.

<u>If you are in the Care Bear stage, transformation is possible if:</u>

- You can play a bigger game. There's a banquet being offered and you deserve the best. Dig in and enjoy.
- Ask for help in qualifying people for your business. Sometimes because we want to help, we do not see clearly.
- You do some leadership training and personal development to see yourself as deserving to attract and work with more successful people. All people can benefit from your generosity of spirit.
- You stop your fixing habit. You do not need to mother people.

I can relate to Care Bears, especially because in the beginning, I wanted to fix everyone until I woke up to what I was doing. I pretty quickly realized they didn't need fixing; they were perfectly happy being in the place they were in and didn't require any interference from me. One of the traps I used to fall into was wanting success for others more than they did. I easily see people's potential and when invited, I love to support them to bring their gifts and talents into their business. I have learned that success can be measured so differently for each one of us. The bottom line for me is how happy a person is at the end of the day. There is no point in killing yourself to get somewhere, when you're not having fun and you don't feel inspired. Not everyone needs to be at the top levels to feel totally successful. Care Bears are not so interested in the extrinsic goals in life.

You have to find out what your Care Bears want and need. Find out if they're ready for change. And are they ready now? (See Chapter 21: Journey from Willingness to Readiness.) Keep in mind also that they live to serve and what they call success, another person may not. What is important is what *they* want.

Care Bears genuinely want to play a support role and they really do not look for recognition. In fact, they feel quite uncomfortable when they are singled out or praised. They prefer to be quite invisible if they can.

I had so much to learn about this category because I always thought success meant getting to the top of the levels and receiving recognition, etc. My Care Bears have taught me about selfless service. The real Care Bears are without ego or at least very little. I strive to be more like them in this way.

Chapter 4

Cats — *Entitled*

Most Cats, when they read this, will rarely recognize themselves. They are likely to skim through this section, thinking it must be about someone else. Cats have a bit of an entitlement attitude. You can ask Cats to do something but you cannot tell them to. They often appear as if they have it all together. Maybe they do.

Cats are definitely clever, intuitive, and instinctive. They are independent (though often needy), authentic, and a little wild. You would love to have a Cat on your team if you could only tame him or her. The point is that you can't, so stop trying. Instead work with Cats' strengths, which are focus, perseverance, and patience.

You may think that you have caught a Cat but really, he or she has caught you. Isn't that a surprise? Unlike Dogs, they have little, if no desire to please anyone, so take it as a compliment when they come and sit on your lap. Secretly though, they do love their assorted family members.

Cats are some of the most difficult members of the team because they're un-coachable and contrary in many ways. Sometimes they are a little too dramatic and think a situation is a CATastrophe, when really it is not.

However they're unique and amazing hunters, so you want them on your team. It's clear that most of the other Team members are happy either to be a leader, or to have a pack leader. Dog loves having a master, Sheep loves its shepherd but the Cat prefers to have staff! It's as simple as that.

Cats are a little out of step with most other people's schedules; for instance, being nocturnal. Often, when the group is going in one direction, they are going in the other. They love their catnaps and lounging around. Some may call it lazy — they call it conserving energy. They often forget appointments because they don't use calendars. When they return or wake up, they may find themselves lost and confused. In this business, you have to stay abreast of what's happening on your team and be current.

This distancing behaviour can be interpreted as aloof, self-absorbed, and disinterested. In reality, Cats do care but their instincts often get the better of them.

Isolated and alone is where they put themselves in their wounded state (especially Scaredy Cats) and they can disappear for long periods of time. This fearful and cautious place may come across as critical and sometimes aggressive — or worse, passive aggressive. This can be hard for Cats and it can be hard to be around, so the separation they create is often a relief. Trust this and be patient with them until they feel safe to come out again.

Since Cats are not pack animals per se, it's almost foreign for them to get behind others in a real and consistent way. Cats may be better supporters; taking on one person at a time. Just as you cannot herd cats, they do not like herding others either. This is why they are not the strongest leaders. To be a "coach" will be a learned behaviour for Cats, rather than an instinctive behaviour. So be patient and show them how.

Attempting to get them to lead their team or go for a certain goal can be challenging. The moment they think you are trying to control them, they pull back, hiss at you, and hide. In this way, they are unpredictable because just when you think all is going well, out of the blue can come complete resistance. This is why you cannot depend heavily on them. You have to get behind their motives and their vision, to bring out the best in them in a careful way so you don't spook them. But when they do engage, they are masters of precision and you will be pleasantly surprised by what they find or whom they find.

Cats may not be easy contributors to your Team but if you take on the challenge of Cat, persevere and stay the course with them; there are many gifts in store. They are great teachers because they show you that while it's a business of duplication, the new currency today is authenticity. If you can learn to work with Cats and bring out their gifts and talents, then they will be really solid players on your team.

What you can learn from Cats:

- Precision and patience when looking for key people to join your team.
- A quiet confidence. They do not apologize for being themselves. Nor should you.
- They know how to take a good catnap during the day and relax.

How to enthuse Cats:

- Be ready when they are ready to hang out.
- Create a way to help them to shine in their strengths.
- Give them tons of space to be themselves.
- Praise and pet them, they love it.
- Reassure them often that their contribution counts.

- Watch out not to put your expectations on them.

<u>If you recognize yourself in the Cat stage, transformation is possible if:</u>

- You first of all admit it.
- You stop pussyfooting around and become coachable.
- You become consistent and reliable.
- You get a calendar and start using it
- You're willing to move out of your comfort zone.
- You recognize that in terms of the team, the Cat way is a difficult, contrary energy to work with.
- You share your gifts and talents in a way that works for you.
- You listen and learn more about other members of your team.
- You focus outwards on others and ask often, "How may I be of service?"
- You realize that you need more purposeful action in your life. Instead of conserving energy, get outside and connect with wonderful people.

I think of my own cat and he is affectionate, needy, lovable, fluffy, an amazing hunter and a solid member of my family. I'm never confused by his behaviour though. **He does his own thing** but we have an understanding and this is the first step to a really loving relationship. And I am grateful. Like anything, there are exceptions to the rule and a Cat could be coachable. But that is rare and here we are dealing with generalities for the sake of identifying a stuck state that easily can be transformed with willingness.

Chapter 5

Deer — *Innocent*

Deer people are gentle in word, thought, and touch. They are highly sensitive and you have to earn their trust by your awareness of their vulnerability. Deer have a purity of heart and cannot handle cruelty in the world or in your tone. Always approach them with care if you want to get close to them. Deer are alert and aware of what is going on, so you cannot deceive them. Instead you can ask them for their clarity and it is there that you will find Deer's gift.

They are great herd members and like to fit in and play their part. They are not natural leaders, so when Deer step forth, they are being very courageous. Deer in the wild are always on red alert due to the threat of predators. In the business however, Deer tend to worry too much about things they do not need to worry about.

Since Deer are reluctant leaders you may have to assign them into roles they wouldn't volunteer for. By you believing in them and offering them opportunities to shine, they will grow and they want to grow. Just because Deer are gentle, doesn't mean they cannot get things done. They have mastered the art of determination in their gentle approach.

Deer will never push, as they know the balance of true power is in gentleness and compassion.

However you don't want to underestimate the powers of Deer. If provoked or needing to protect another, they may turn aggressive. It is rare and it is not the norm for Deer but it is possible when the chips are down. Always remember that the power of the stag is within, and it can be magnificent and a force to reckon with.

Deer have more instinctive fear than most other members because, similar to horses, they are flight animals. They do better in the herd than out-there alone and to them survival is about how fast they can run from a threatening scene. You may not find them alone in coffee shops looking for prospects. Instead let them find their own way of meeting potential partners. It will probably be unique.

Don't expect your Deer to be confrontational. If a difficult incident arises in the Tribe, they will not be the first ones to speak up because of a fear of being seen or making a mistake. A mistake for a deer could cost it its life. They will be extremely affected if things are not in harmony and will usually disappear or retreat from the business until they feel safe enough to come out again. This creates inconsistency, with which it is hard to build a business and it is impossible to lead. In this aspect, Deer are similar to Cats.

Deer like to live simple lives and they have a hard time adjusting to unpredictable situations. They don't like change and want everything to stay the same if possible. Instinctively however, Deer are designed for change. Deer have a vigilance, which gives them the ability to change directions quickly.

Deer teach us that adaptability is imperative. Today, in any business, change is inevitable so it is better to embrace it and do what you need to do to feel secure within it. Maybe you need more information or maybe you will need to speak up. Take care of your needs so that you don't become whiney or a victim.

Deer are gentle spirits, clear minded and have an air of innocence about them. They have to feel very safe in order to allow themselves to be visible. If going up to the next business promotion means that they will be getting up on stage, they will need a lot of hand holding as becoming visible in this way is not natural for Deer. It is outside their comfort zone. In order to find ease, they would have to forge their way ahead by clearly being out of their comfort zones on a regular basis. After all, courage and comfort cannot co-exist. The beauty of Relationship Marketing's particular business model is that they don't have to be out there being seen until they are ready. There are many other members of the Tribe who are happy to be at the front of the pack or at the front of the stage. Like every animal group here, you will have a shy one, a confident one, an audacious one and more.

Within each characteristic or stage can come great healing. The more we step forward with courage, the more our limitations reveal themselves to be cleared. You don't have to worry about what people will think or do when your heart is filled with love. Your inner love is your protection. It's not only your protection, it's your greatest gift.

<u>What you can learn from Deer:</u>

- How to speak kindly and clearly about others.
- How to be a great herd member and watch out for others.
- How to increase your awareness in communication — to pay close attention to what is happening around you.

<u>How to enthuse Deer:</u>

- Connect with them carefully and truthfully.
- Bring out their gifts and talents (they may not know what they are).
- Speak in a gentle and loving tone, with respect.
- Graze beside them in the field.
- Never push but gently nudge them in a new direction.

<u>If you recognize yourself in the Deer stage, transformation is possible if :</u>

- You get used to change. It's happening all the time.
- You relax, don't run away so quickly
- You are courageous and step out of your comfort zone.
- You practice leading others — you do have what it takes.
- You trust yourself more and know you are supported.
- You are supportive of others; this will help you with your fear.
- You think outside the field.
- You share your sacred peacefulness — the world needs you.
- You share your gift of clarity with your team.

Yes I have had to learn how to work with Deer and it is a delicate matter. Seeing potential and wanting to hurry them along faster than they are ready to go can be frustrating. This has gotten me into a lot of trouble and in many cases I have alienated my Deer.

I am now learning to work with Deer gently, encouraging them to come out to play because they have so much clarity and love to offer. We need them in our Tribe for it to be complete. Deer can shine bright and blow you away with their ability when you least expect it.

Chapter 6

Dog — *Loyal*

Dog nature is loyal, consistent, happy, and generous. With faithfulness and protection at their core, they are serving humanity. They are honest, trustworthy, kind, and very friendly. They love to please and don't need to be the centre of attention (all the time that is) — they make everyone else in the team the important ones. Dogs do not complain and find joy in every little thing. They are willing and happy to support with whatever is needed. You want as many of these in your pack as you can find. Dogs have an acute sense of smell and can sniff out insincerity a mile away. But their generous disposition will always see the best in others first and lick them into their goodness if at all possible.

In this business, many components are repetitious and people fall away quickly because of this. Not Dogs though, they will eat the same kibble and go on the same walks every day with as much vigour, joy, and gusto, as if for the first time. Dogs are the masters of this. Learn from them how to surrender to the fact that repetition is a part of the game and the more you can do with keenness, the better. Remember it's not about you; instead it's about the brand new person just arriving.

People with this Dog temperament are absolutely coachable and as a result can build a fairly robust and sustainable business. They are totally capable of getting all the way to the top in this business and when they do; they turn around and put all the credit on to the team/pack. They are loyal to their company, their products, and their team and YES they will go the distance with you. Persistence is their middle name and being of service is their joy. They never tire of you and even if you screw up, they look up to you with tenacious enthusiasm and give you a second chance. They will protect you to the end and bark, if necessary, at someone who tries to harm their leader.

How to enthuse Dogs:

What you can learn from Dogs:

- Unconditional love.
- How to be non-judgmental
- To be present in the moment; "the now."
- Not to worry or reflect on the past. To be forgiving.
- To go the distance and not quit.
- To bring fun and play to your work and team.

How to enthuse Dogs:

- Just love them and appreciate their role and abilities.
- Thank them. They do not need this but you do.
- Dogs love gifts — throw them a bone every now and then. *Don't you notice this in dog people? They so appreciatively and joyously receive little gifts.*

If you are in the Dog stage, maybe you're happy where you are. However, if you are ready, transformation is possible if:

- You find out what you want and what you deserve.
- You always do best in a place of serving the pack, so whom can you get behind, to help him or her achieve success? Keep focusing on this and before you know it, you will be very successful but more importantly, you will feel fulfilled.
- You aim higher and ask for more. Often content and accepting of where you are, you may have to up your game and set a *highest and best plan* for yourself. Knowing this will inspire your team — you're willing to be *best in class.*

- You trust your instincts.

I relate to the Dog energy, especially with my retreat centre of nearly twenty years and my Relationship Marketing business of eight years. People say I am like a dog with a bone when I put my mind and heart into something. I always go the distance if it's right and true.

Sometimes Dogs need to step up as distinct leaders and can feel like they are abandoning their packs (which can feel excruciating for Dog). But this is essential to go to the next level. If the pack is ready, it will follow. If not, that's ok, there are other great people along the way to align with. Stepping out of their comfort zones and perhaps feeling a little sadness when they have to leave pack members behind because they're not ready to run with them can be a challenge for dogs. They will be ok if they accept that everyone goes at his or her own speed and time. Many pack members become inspired and run to catch up down the road.

I am currently willing to expand my dream and feel worthy of bringing it forward to the next level. What are you now ready to bring forward?

Chapter 7

Dolphin — *Enthusiastic*

Dolphins are passionate, playful, and community minded. Their sheer enthusiasm propels them forward in this business. They are magnetic and people want to join them. They are the epitome of team spirit — the pod is everything and they work together for the betterment of all. These sensitive and responsive souls are skilled communicators and highly adaptable. They have *the magic and synergy consciousness* and if you can bring one onto your team, you are blessed. You may have to step up your game however, because Dolphins are the real deal and once you bond with them, they are comrades forever. They have a unique diplomacy and the ability to steer away from conflict where possible. For them, it is all about keeping the peace of the pod intact.

Dolphins really know how to be in the flow with life — not taking every little thing personally. They match the rhythm of the business elegantly and effortlessly. Dolphins understand commitment like no other. *They know the irony of commitment is that it's deeply liberating.*

What you can learn from Dolphins:

- Enthusiasm and delight for living — this is attractive to people.
- Sincerity.
- How to be a great pod player — Dolphins love their communities.
- Natural flow — "healing energy."

- Consistency and how small actions each day add up to huge results.

How to enthuse your Dolphins:

- Have fun with them.
- Keep it light and playful.
- Keep it real.
- Commit 100% to your involvement with them.

If you are in the Dolphin stage, just remember:

- You already are the greatest role model.
- To stay on the wave and don't get pulled down by negativity.

I love the playful spirit of Dolphins and how much fun they can seem to have. It reflects to me the importance of keeping a light attitude. Most people want to have fun and will be drawn to us when we are playful. I felt the enthusiasm of the Dolphin stage in the beginning of my business and I love to witness it in new people when they have their first glimpse of what this business could mean for them.

When they catch the wave of possibilities, Dolphins dance with their visions and dreams. Now, I have to remind myself to call upon Dolphin energy whenever I start to take things too seriously and get down on myself, or others. The beautiful thing about Dolphin energy is that Dolphins have endurance and can travel far with you. There are many things in this business that will challenge you, so you have to definitely keep your attitude in check and seek support from your team if you get down. As the saying goes: *"If you are down, go up to your leaders. If you are up, go down and share with your team."*

Dolphin leaders inspire people into success by their willingness to work alongside them, even if they have achieved the level others are working towards. They will simply look to their next level so they can be in action with someone else at the same time. Rather than coaching others to where they are, they are swimming along beside them, towards their next achievement. They have a big capacity, with so much energy, and they enjoy being part of others' success. Dolphins are born to inspire greatness in the world by their very presence. They live life as their highest and best. Do you?

Chapter 8

Eagle — *Visionary Leader*

Eagles are an anomalous group — in the top one-percent. They are visionary and action-oriented. The power of concentration is their secret weapon. They know where they are going and like a straight arrow, they get there.

Usually they are professional MLM/Network Marketers, having had experience in the industry before; their apprenticeship was done (blood, sweat, and tears) in another company first. Once they've found the right company, they will stick to it like glue and make it their personal responsibility for it to succeed. They will go the distance with a company worthy of their strength and ability and will drop one if it is not. When Eagles join your company, their past experience pays off and they will move up through the ranks at lightning speed (top level positions in one — six months). Eagles play a very strategic game and with extraordinary focus and talent, can build a huge team. They've paid their dues, know how the game's played and deserve all the success that comes to them. Please don't compare yourself with this group unless you want to torment yourself. They are rare.

Eagles have the vitality and extraordinary power to create energy and get the job done. They are problem solvers and have no interest in blame or small talk. These individuals thrive on the challenges that many others fear and avoid. They will champion you but don't expect them to be warm and fuzzy. Secretly they have tender hearts but may not show you that side very often, unless it is purposeful.

Eagles fly high and are not afraid of being disliked. They lead until you show up and lead. They have the power to change the entire game because they are courageous and clear leaders. They are focused visionaries and will not waste time on meaning-less endeavours or people who pretend to be willing, able, and ready to fly with them. They will test you and see how high you can really fly. True Eagles will never be your boss but will offer challenges to empower you... leading by their own example. As mentors, Eagles are known for being soft on their people but hard on the issues that compromise their success.

They naturally engender an environment of trust, which allows people to believe in them and follow instructions where necessary.

If you attract any into your business — you had better get rein-forcements to support them at their level.

<u>What you can learn from Eagles:</u>

- How to lead. Watch them and follow what they do.
- How to stand in the gap when your company needs you to.
- How to see and trust the bigger picture.
- How to set the bar high and keep it there.

<u>How to enthuse Eagles:</u>

- Everyone likes to be seen and acknowledged, even if they are very successful. Eagles are no exception.
- Be sincere and never try to embarrass them.

- Go the distance. Don't waste their time.
- Step up to the plate and play the best game you can with them.

<u>If you are soaring the skies, thank you for being an inspiration:</u>

- Keep an open heart and remember people need your mentoring.
- Remember your role is to be a beacon of light and hope for others.
- Stay in integrity every step of the way.
- Work on sustainability because your ability and vision are big.

I have had the pleasure of working with Eagles and what I love about them is how they do not lower the bar, no matter what. They are masters at holding people accountable and they will never ask you to do anything they are not willing to do or have not already done. Trust Eagles, they will take you to high places if you are ready.

Chapter 9

Hare — *Erratic*

In fast and out fast is the name of Hares' game. They may be incredibly bright and enthusiastic at first but this energy dwindles rapidly once they see how much work is involved. Hares usually join your team because they're interested in a "get rich quick scheme." They tend to be big talkers with little action and get discouraged quickly. They want to earn $10,000 per month as quickly as possible but put in $200 worth of effort and expect to succeed. Just when they begin to receive a little success — they say it's not moving fast enough and vanish from sight.

In the beginning, they attract people fairly easily but it is usually short-lived because they are not really engaged. Hares have a kind of commitment phobia because they do not trust. Their behaviour is erratic and hard to depend on. They say they will show up and they do for a while but then, out of nowhere, they stop and disappear. Because they do have power of influence (at least in the beginning) they disturb their teams by darting from one thing to another with much conviction. They talk about their latest greatest scheme, calling it "the greatest thing in the world." Then, when they see something shiny in another direction, they jump ship once again. It can be difficult for you when they leave and unfortunately, this profession attracts many Hares, which doesn't help the industry's reputation.

Hares are not loyal to any particular company or mission — they seem to have trouble making the connection and then don't follow through all the way. This doesn't make them bad people;

it's just a pattern that runs their lives until they become aware and choose differently. I think deep down they would love to be a part of something really meaningful but they do not have the horsepower or discipline to stay long enough to ground it. They lose credibility with the team fast.

Ironically, Hares often realize in hindsight that they have made a very big mistake by not sticking with one company and putting down roots. Not all is lost for the team however, providing you work with any members that they brought in. Offer your services right away to members who want to stay and succeed and treat them as if you sponsored them. It is industry practice to reach down and support people who come into your business, no matter who brought them in.

How you can learn from Hares:

- How to be light-hearted and not take things so seriously.
- To be ambitious and optimistic.
- How compulsive *early adopters* waste a lot of time and energy.
- What commitment phobia looks like.

How to enthuse Hares:

- See if you can trip them up as they're running by (gently of course).
- Get to know them and find out what they are really interested in.
- Be the grounding for them so they can centre themselves and stay.

If you are in the Hare stage, transformation is possible if:

- YOU **STOP**, LOOK & LISTEN: Find a company that is legitimate and inspiring and glue your feet to the ground. Do not even look at anything else for three to five years. Find your deepest passion and then find other people who share similar dreams. Stay with your team. Stay with your company and stay with your vision, no matter what happens.

- You learn to say "No" to addictive patterns and reactions.
- You ask for help and then have the respect to take it and learn from it. Ask Beaver for help and watch and emulate their activity.
- You learn what commitment and loyalty mean — you may even like it. Speak to Dog.
- You are willing and ready to have another run at it. What have you got to lose? You could have a lot to gain.

I have experienced the Hare who leaves before success or on the brink of success. I understand this conduct is part of the industry experience. Sometimes though, a sincere seeker of a brilliant business venture will land at the feet of a really worthwhile company and together they can begin to grow. I have had to learn how to handle the disappointment that comes with Hare behaviour and you can read more about how to take care of disappointment in Chapter 25. I suggest you move on and continue to work with people who are ready to commit.

Before joining this profession, I definitely related to the Hare mind-set, in both my work and relationships. I would drive my friends and family crazy as I flitted from one thing to another, with full-on conviction that it was the way, or that *he* was the one, only to drop them and move to the next important thing. I give thanks to my work with Instinx[2], which helped me to grow my capacity to stay grounded, focused, and able to succeed in a very big way.

Transforming from Hare has been so wonderful and I am truly grateful. Sometimes you don't know what you don't know and this exercise is all about bringing awareness to a situation.

---

2   Griffin, Gus, www.Instinx.com

Chapter 10

Horse — *Born to Run*

I have lived with and around horses since the age of six and my heart and soul are opened in profound ways just by being in their presence. They know exactly what is going on and can read you like a book. You cannot fake it or hide your feelings from them because they are tuned in to you not only on instinctive levels but on what appears to be psychic levels too.

Horses can read your energy, your motive, and your mood. Horses are the perfect mirrors in which to see yourself. They are the real teachers.

Horses are a precocial species, which basically means they hit the ground running. (Precocial refers to species in which the young are relatively mature and mobile from the moment of birth.)

They don't wait to be trained; they get going and learn along the way. With energy that's very similar to Dolphins' energy, Horses are popular members within your team. They are playful, intelligent, charismatic, and born to run. Don't try to lasso them into your business — that was the way of the old paradigm. They value their indomitable surge towards FREEDOM. No need to break their spirit by leashing/training them, instead gentle them in and let them catch you. Let them come to you when they're ready and leave them to roam beside you freely. They will watch you for a while before they decide to join. Their need for harmony and balance is paramount in the herd.

Let them come to you because they're curious and interested in what you have to offer. Horses are open-minded, trustworthy, confident, and very friendly. They are unique and quite different from each other in many ways. They will teach you how to handle them.

You'd better leave your ego at the side of the field when approaching Horses because they're not interested in inauthentic behaviour and they command honesty every step of the way. They will respect you if you treat them kindly.

They are smart and tuned in, with an immense sensitivity and you can learn so much from them because of this. They can be great leaders and great followers alike, which makes them a considerable gift to your Team. They are purpose-driven and really want to do a good job. When they make the connection to a bigger purpose they could well be your top achievers since they have a power of influence and the horsepower to pull it off. They don't mind being the centre of attention or one of the herd — either way they are magical.

Their strength and speed is vast and they have the stamina to carry you and your team far. Since horses are flight animals you cannot make them do something they do not understand. If they are afraid, they will run away and ask questions later. Therefore you have to listen to them and learn their language so they will understand. When they trust you, they are highly coachable and in many ways will be the ones doing the coaching. Working with them in partnership is awesome.

Remember the saying: you can lead a horse to water but you cannot make it drink. This is true if you are trying to make Horses do something they have not yet bought into. You cannot coerce Horses and that's for sure; they will see through you with lightning speed. They can, however, be enticed with a little bit of apple and some kind words. Make sure as a leader, you show them by doing something first. Lead them and they will follow happily.

If you feel like you are spinning your wheels and not able to build traction in your business, observe horse. Success leaves clues and loves speed and so do horses. There's nothing more exciting to me than working with people who have the stamina, fortitude and capacity to really go for it.

What you can learn from Horses:

- To be totally honest with yourself and others.
- To run like the wind and build a business fast.
- To be clear about the energy you are bringing into the herd. (Check your ego at the gate before entering the paddock.)

How to enthuse Horses:

- Be transparent — they can read you anyway.
- Be consistent and dependable.
- Approach with a still mind.
- Be kind.
- Be trustworthy, so they can be themselves.
- With softness, everything is available all the time.
- Explain well your motive and actions.

If you are in the Horse stage, transformation is possible if:

- You check to see what is really happening before you take off.
- You offer your talent and skills; there are many.
- You offer your sensitivity and strength to the team.
- You focus on developing others in your herd, to be able to do what you do so effortlessly.
- You show patience with all members of your team who may not be moving as fast as you.
- You become a little more coachable and willing to rein it in a bit.

- At the same time, you unleash your full horsepower.

Often you will find really strong herd leaders and when you do, you want to make sure you have your saddle strapped on tight because they can run as fast as the wind and leave you standing in the dust. In the industry, it is often referred to as a "runaway leg." Make no mistake though, I am not suggesting slowing them down — I am saying, stay abreast of them if you can and you will have the ride of your life.

Everything is about energy and resonance. What you say, how you look, and what you think all play a part in the vibration emanating from you.

Imagine if all your new potential partners were able to read your energy and could tell if you have an agenda or are afraid of rejection or judgment. It's subtle and delicate yet if you can master this, it is transformative. So how do we do this?

By becoming aware of your thoughts and feelings. I cannot believe how many people are completely unaware that they have a dialogue yakking away all day long inside their heads and do not hear it. The beginning of awareness is sometimes shocking when you start to actually hear what you are saying to yourself. In fact we would never speak to our worst enemies the way we sometimes speak to ourselves. Our feelings are potent manufacturers of reality and we have to really tune into our bodies and minds to find out what is going on. There are many other chapters in this book that will guide you to greater levels of awareness.

As a fun aside, I thought I'd share a metaphor for how we usually do this business on a monthly basis — not just Horses but most members of the tribe. From giddy up to whoa looks like this:

Week 1. WALK. Resting, relaxing, mingling, taking a breath, and reviewing previous month, coffee dates. Setting new plans and intentions.

Week 2. TROT — Follow-ups; training; inviting and connecting with new potential partners.

Week 3. CANTER. Loping along, faster but smoother, in your stride. Happiness, ease, and grace.

Week 4. GALLOP (Otherwise referred to as: end of the month.) Flat-out running and going for it to meet deadlines.

For whatever reason, that is the rhythm of this business and as much as we try to get the work done at the beginning of the month, it inevitably ends up this way. Horses of course, love to gallop at the beginning, middle or end.

Chapter 11

Lone Wolf — *Elusive*

Unlike Dogs or Dolphins, Lone Wolves prefer to be alone. Yet Wolves are some of the most community-minded members there are. When Wolves break away from their packs and become Lone Wolves, their energy becomes out of balance. When Wolves separate out for one reason or another, it affects their ability to relate. In that state, they are not real collaborators.

I have noticed Lone Wolves are often professionals who have had previous success on another career path. These individuals, who have put in years of studying and tons of money earning degrees and maybe even decades in their careers, are finding their way to this industry. It may take time for them to step forward but when they do, be professional with them and respect their sensibilities. Show them how Relationship Marketing is a great and worthy Profession. They could be a contender.

You will find Lone Wolves showing up at events now and again, checking things out but staying relatively on the periphery of things. A similar concept is the Lone Wolf of a particular group, who spends enough time with a group to be considered a member but not enough time to be very close to the other members. Such people tend to not take part in the group activities or "get-togethers."

You will often find Lone Wolves aloof and reluctant to commit to the overall team. They are intellectuals and get caught analyzing themselves right out of the picture. They may be in the room but they are often busy with their thoughts, iPhone or some other more important distraction. If they get as far as recruiting people, they start managing them and not connecting them to the greater infrastructure of support that's available. They tend to think the buck stops with them, which was the paradigm they came from. In many ways they're not quite sure how the game is played, since they are not usually open to the training being offered. It may work for a while but the disconnect will eventually create difficulty and weariness.

Relationship Marketing is not a game of Solitaire. It activates when two or more come together in synergy, just like you cannot light a fire with nothing but a single log. Lone Wolves tend to be more critical than others, perhaps a little perfectionistic, which can be really hard to be around and not very appealing.

Lone Wolves basically have a fear of committing and want only to put a paw in. As a result, there is no real connection or intimacy, and we never really get to know him or her, and vice versa. One of my mentors tells me that if you have Lone Wolves in your pack, in many ways they have already left. Unless of course, you can help them to see that they are playing at the periphery of the game, which is no game.

What you can learn from Lone Wolves:

- The importance of working with your Pack.
- Wolves are imbued with ambition and virtue. Learn from them.

How to enthuse Lone Wolves:

- Let them know you see them. Keep inviting them to join the team.
- Remind them of the true community spirit.
- Ask them to play a role in the team so they have to participate.
- Honour their competence.

<u>If you are at the Lone Wolf stage, transformation is possible if:</u>

- You are willing to run with the Pack. This means being coachable and part of the team structure, where you show up with your strengths and talents consistently.
- You join the team fully — stop separating yourself.
- You understand that you can do this business part-time successfully, or full-time successfully, but you cannot do it *sometimes* successfully.
- You get off your solo professional high horse and realize this is an entirely different business model, which has the ability to grow to massive proportions, and for which duplication is the name of the game.
- You understand that in order to have time freedom, you cannot be the manager but you can be a pack leader.
- You stop over-analyzing everything. Make a decision and take action.
- You make a strong commitment to the team.

I definitely can relate to being non-committal in other areas of my life — kind of on the outside, looking in; wanting to join but not sure if this is my tribe. I highly recommend doing whatever research and due diligence is needed (don't overdo it though), to get clear and then look to the successful ones in your business and find out how the culture of the business works. There are all shapes, sizes, and levels of backgrounds and breeds. Join your pack — together you can make a big difference and support each other in ways you may not have ever imagined.

If you identify with the Lone Wolf, your leadership qualities and skill base are huge and once you see how the game is played — you will understand what a contribution you can make to the team, to the company, and to the world. Plus, this business is an excellent training ground for relationships and collaboration.

Chapter 12

Lynx — *Seer*

Many will not relate to Lynx for Lynx are mysterious and unknown in many ways.

These resplendent creatures are lucid and serve the invisible rules of this business. Lynx have the gift of seeing and strong intuitive intelligence. They are focused hunters.

There are two sides to Lynx. One: is what they see and the road maps they carry within. Two: is the way they work in the world with a kind of *dancing between the molecules* effect. They know you don't have to expend a ton of energy to get results. The old paradigm of stacking up your calendar and talking to hundreds of people, to find one, is not the way of the Lynx. In fact it is the reverse — talking to one to find a hundred. Lynx adhere to the philosophy of: *Do less — achieve more*. This doesn't mean they're lazy or copping out of work. It means they guard their time and energy and when they use it, it is precise and on target. As a result, they build their business almost invisibly. This is very different than Lone Wolves, who definitely separate out from others and start managing. Lynx have no desire to manage anyone. Instead these individuals are present and do the obvious things one must do in their business. Yet something else is going on beneath the surface that most cannot fathom.

In many ways, what Lynx do is seamless and you barely notice their actions but if you pay close attention and you have the awareness, you will learn much from them. It may even take Lynx people a while to understand this power of intuition because it is so effortless for them. They may never have understood it as a gift or something special.

Lynx bring the invisible into the visible by their keen observation and this is their secret and their magic. People who carry this energy and may have been sitting on it for years, are now being encouraged, nudged even, to share what it is they see. Our world is changing; our consciousness is changing and Lynx know the indiscernible way of this business. In many cases, people with this Lynx energy have been oppressed or were guarded growing up. In some cases, they might have been called weird or witch-like and as a result, they have learned to keep their mouths shut and not share what it is that they see.

Do not expect Lynx to show up at the Monday morning board meeting and don't approach them with a wordy strategic plan because they operate more from what's happening in the moment. Lynx act instinctively and that is their teaching. Don't expect them to follow your rules, fill out application forms, or write copious notes and distribute them edited. They dance to the beat of their own drums, yet they still get the job done and this is what you have to recognize. If you're going to get caught up expecting your rules to be adhered to, then you're barking up the wrong tree. If you start demanding that of your Lynx, you are probably going to lose them or get exhausted trying to get them to meet your expectations. Let them operate instinctively and allow them to work in their strengths. Watch them and learn from them. And do not watch on the surface because it is below the surface that they function.

They can see in the dark and can see through you into your blind spots. Darkness being the unconscious patterns and beliefs that may be playing havoc in your life. They will not share this with you but you can probably pry it out of them if you ask.

If you resonate with Lynx, they will show you the way. There is so much more yet to see and understand for all of us. If you do not resonate, you will barely read these words and that's the beauty of this complex Tribe. We can all be different and yet co-operate within a common mission.

Lynx people work with their intuition and the more they rely on this, the stronger it becomes. Just as a muscle gets stronger with use, so does the intuition until such a point that you can trust it implicitly, even when it seems ridiculous to do so. Without use, it atrophies like any other muscle. It's because this sixth sense is so highly developed in Lynx, that people don't understand how Lynx can see things that they cannot. The gift of *seeing*, everyone has, but he or she has to choose to develop it.

Although Lynx seem serious, they have a sense of spontaneous, kittenish, light-hearted play when you least expect it. They can really bring out the child-like qualities in the team. The lighter and more fun you are, the easier it is to attract others to your team.

Nothing escapes Lynx's watchful gaze for long. They pay attention to what people do, rather than what they say and they base their decisions on that. This business is saturated with people who are dreamers. But unfortunately, not everyone follows his or her dream to completion. Some people lack follow- through or give up way too easily. Lynx love to witness those who are really ready to go the distance and step forward in their power. Lynx find passion in guiding and playing with them, as they create a substantial business together.

If you want to find out why you are creating the same problems over and over again, ask Lynx. It takes a rare soul, however, to seek out Lynx, for their seeing. This is because most of us prefer to hide within the shell of our own dogma, which Lynx is able to penetrate with cutting accuracy.

Lynx people are usually introverted and need time and space alone to recharge their batteries. It doesn't usually take long; even twenty minutes in nature can make all the difference. Sitting by a tree or listening to nature sounds settles them down into a peaceful way of being. While they are very capable of being out in the world with a strong presence, it is fundamental to their nature that they retreat regularly to regroup. They understand that doing their own deep inner work is necessary to be of service in a clear and effective way.

Technology is a powerful tool, now available in the world. High touch and high tech is the rhythm of Lynx. And yes, what a perfect vehicle to use; Relationship Marketing.

What you can learn from Lynx:

- To see your gifts and talents by asking them to share what they see.
- To connect to your higher self for answers and solutions.
- To learn the art of doing less and achieving more by purposeful actions.
- To stay away from expending unnecessary energy on drama
- How to qualify potential partners.

How to enthuse Lynx:

- Look at their results, rather than what you think they should be doing.
- Be curious about their methodology.
- Give them plenty of space.
- Let them work in their strength and fill in the details for them.
- Be playful with them — they love to have fun.

If you are at the Lynx stage, transformation is possible if:

- You share your gifts with discretion.

- You open up to the systems available — they will not bite you.
- You trust that structures are useful and important.
- You realize that not everyone thinks and sees the way you do, so in order to duplicate what you do, you may have to interpret your language.
- You take time alone to contemplate and regroup.
- You trust your own knowing and seeing.

For Lynx, their lives are paths of faith, trust, and great courage. Sometimes they are guided to do things that do not make logical sense. But do them they must. The result of tuning in and acting from this level is always propitious. In spite of unusual characteristics, a person with Lynx energy can build a highly successful business in the "REAL" world…and we know what real really means.

In many ways Lynx are the most unique animals in the Tribe because there is little known about their ways. I relate to Lynx and have been surprised in writing this, how much I am learning about myself.

Chapter 13

Mouse — *Plays a Small Game*

Mice live by the status quo, doing their jobs and fretting about the details of what is needed and where to get it. They tend to be fixated on tiny, weeny minutiae and worried about survival. A Mouse's top priority is gathering what is needed for the winter. A virtuous Mouse is constantly thinking and calculating what is fair and what is not. Mice pride themselves on having a well-organized and full calendar but this leaves little room for spontaneity and freedom. Their flexibility is compromised because everything is scheduled in their world. It also limits what can be accomplished.

Mice tend to be picky, sometimes criticizing and being paranoid about things that are irrelevant to the bigger picture. They do not see the bigger picture and do not trust well, due to their limited vision. After all, Mice barely see beyond the blades of grass. It is a vulnerable position to be in and Mice know this well.

Mice usually stay within a small network of friends and family, preferring to stay close to home and rarely branching out to other lands. In most cases their Mouse community is all they really know. They often stay in the same tedious job or relationship for way too long. Mice play a small game and live a small life, not realizing so much more is possible. Even if they realize it, they don't believe enough in themselves to go for it.

Every now and again you will attract an audacious Mouse willing to go beyond known reality to investigate new possibilities. When this inner call beckons, he or she no longer can resist the pull and finally leaves home base. It takes courage to begin and faith to continue. Then, low and behold, his or her true power is discovered.

I cannot help but insert a very special story here that will relate to this audacious mouse.

Jumping Mouse[3] is a beautiful Native American story of courage, compassion, and luminosity. I would like to share a shortened version of the story because it speaks volumes about taking the initiative to go beyond your boundaries. Many other members of the Tribe may relate to this story as well so pull up your chair.

Once upon a time, there was a really busy Mouse. He loved moving things around from one place to another. He was an upstanding member of the community and there was something just a little bit different about him. For years this particular little mouse heard a distant sound in his ears. When he asked the other mice if they heard it too, they said, "No." They were blunt and discouraging and ignored his incessant questioning. Being a good Mouse, he stayed within the confines of his village, keeping busy with this and that, for a very long time.

This compelling sound intrigued him and wouldn't let him rest. It insisted on Little Mouse's attention by day and by night. Eventually, his curiosity pried him lose and he found himself heading towards the distant roaring sound. He knew the risk of being taken by the black shadows that moved across the skies. However he was more inspired by this deep inner prompting that stirred and moved his very being.

You can imagine how scared and alone Little Mouse was as he turned his back on his community and scurried out into the night, across the forest floor. Prayers of survival kept his mind occupied. Little did he know it would be a long and perilous journey.

---

3   Storm, Hyemeyohsts. *Seven Arrows*. Ballantine Books, 1985

Early the next morning, Little Mouse heard a shuffling behind a bush. Turning around, he was startled when he saw Raccoon.

"Hello Little Mouse. What are you doing so far from your home?" inquired Raccoon.

"Oh, you see I'm trying to find the source of this roaring noise that I hear in my ears," said Little Mouse.

"Why that's the river. It is powerful and you will need a guide to take you there," exclaimed Raccoon. "Allow me," he promptly added.

So off they went deeper into the forest and out through a small clearing before tucking in quickly behind some thistles and shrubs. As they made their approach toward the sound, it was deafening and Little Mouse could feel his heart pounding faster and faster. The anticipation was so great that Little Mouse thought he would explode with excitement. Finally, they peered through a bank of long grasses and right in front of them was the mighty river. Mouse was flabbergasted at what he was witnessing.

Raccoon shouted loudly in order to be heard: "I will introduce you to the keeper of the river. His name is Frog. He sits upon that lily pad over there."

Raccoon introduced Little Mouse to Frog and then went on his way to be the guide for others who might be looking for the river.

Little Mouse sat with Frog awhile, taking in the experience of the impressive rushing river.

After a while Frog turned to Little Mouse and asked, "Are you ready for the gift of medicine power?"

"What is that?" asked Little Mouse. Before Frog could answer, little Mouse blurted out, "Yes, yes I am..."

Frog told Little Mouse to come to the edge of the river. He told Little Mouse to crouch down, jump as high as he could and let him know what he saw.

Since Little Mouse was good at following instructions, he crouched down and jumped higher than he had ever jumped before. Mesmerized, he saw a great mountain in the far-off distance. Little Mouse knew this must be the sacred mountain he had heard of. It was more beautiful than anything he had ever seen. Little Mouse wanted to stay there forever but suddenly he felt gravity bring him back to earth with a splash. To his surprise, he landed right in the river and choked on the water. In a panic, he scampered out as fast as his little legs could carry him, trying to catch his breath. At first he was furious with Frog and said, "You have tricked me, I'm all wet."

"Oh relax little fellow, you will be fine but what did you see?" teased Frog.

"Wow... I saw the Sacred Mountain. It does exist." Little Mouse took a moment and then continued, "I want to go there but first I will return to my village and tell my family what I have seen."

"Before you go Little Mouse," said Frog, "you must know you have a new name. Your name is now Jumping Mouse."

In awe, Jumping Mouse returned to his village so excited to share the news. When he arrived, he gathered everyone around him in a little circle. "Come, come," he said. "I have to share with you what I have seen. There is such a thing as a River and she is mighty and has powerful medicine, and beyond that is the Sacred Mountain. They truly do exist for I have seen them with my very own eyes." He shared in detail what he had seen with so much enthusiasm.

Scanning around for some curiosity, he noticed the look of disdain on their faces.

"You are wet Little Mouse and this can only mean that you were in the mouth of a predator," said Brother Mouse. And then he added, "To be spat out like that, you must be filled with poison."

Sister Mouse continued, "Since you are now a threat to this community, you must leave. You no longer belong in this family." She spoke in a scornful tone.

Jumping Mouse was devastated and kept pleading with someone to believe him. Instead, he was banished from his home. Forlorn, he left once again towards the river. This time he did not have a guide to show him the way and he suffered greatly with the distress of being cast out from what he knew to be his life. Days passed and weeks passed and Jumping Mouse became thinner and weaker until early one morning, he came upon a familiar sight.

It was an old Mouse twitching his whiskers and preening himself by the river. Jumping Mouse was so happy to see one of his kin. Old Mouse welcomed Jumping Mouse and invited him into his luxurious home with big twigs, dried leaves and all kinds of other things. Jumping Mouse could see Old Mouse really had established himself well and was living a great life. Everything he needed, including abundant food and shelter, was all around him.

Over a cup of berry juice, Old Mouse told Jumping Mouse that there really wasn't a Sacred Mountain. It was just a story made up by the people of the land. He invited Jumping Mouse to make his home there with him. Old Mouse offered to show him how to get the respect of the mice community back. He said Jumping Mouse would have a fine life and that he would gladly entertain him with stories. He said this was as good as it got. Of course Jumping Mouse was tempted but in his heart of hearts, he knew he wasn't going to be seduced into staying. There was something deeper guiding him forward. He thanked Old Mouse for his hospitality and headed off once again toward his dream.

"Stop you fool, you will be eaten alive out there," Old Mouse shouted after him.

Jumping Mouse did not listen and once again was alone but he was even more convinced he would one day know the Sacred Mountain. He travelled slowly from one cranny to another, watching carefully overhead for the flying black shadows.

One day, as he was contemplating his fate, he saw a big shaggy lump up ahead. It seemed to be moving ever so slightly. Jumping Mouse navigated his way around this enormous unexplainable thing. Aghast, he found that it was a living being, in pain. It was Buffalo.

"Buffalo, you are such a great being but you look sick, what has happened to you?" asked Jumping Mouse.

"I am dying and the only medicine that will cure me is the eye of a mouse and I don't know of any mouse that would give of their eye for me…"

Jumping Mouse was shocked and nervous at first but went away to consider this dilemma. Although he was scared, he knew he could not let this great being die when he had the solution. He finally said, "Yes you may have my eye…" and within a split second, his eye shot out of its socket into the heart of Buffalo.

After a short while, this enormous beast came to his feet and shook, stretched and let out a cry of relief and happiness. He thanked Jumping Mouse and asked what he could do to repay the sacrifice he had made.

Jumping Mouse asked if he would help him get to the Sacred Mountain. Buffalo said he would shelter him from the shadows in the sky if Jumping Mouse tucked in under his belly. Together they journeyed across the great prairie. It took a very long time, but finally they reached the base of the Sacred Mountain.

"This is as far as I can take you, dear Jumping Mouse, but if you continue on up the mountain you will find a guide to take you the rest of the way," said Buffalo. They said their goodbyes and parted ways.

Jumping Mouse was now even thinner and weaker, and so vulnerable with one eye missing. Yet something undeniable kept him moving forward up the mountain, in spite of the fear and loneliness he felt.

For a very long time, he survived on what he could find to eat. He moved slowly by night up the Sacred Mountain until the point where he felt like he just couldn't go on any longer. Then out of nowhere, he came upon a Lone Wolf.

"Brother Wolf," said Jumping Mouse.

He startled the wolf, who jumped in surprise at seeing the mouse. "Hello. Who are you?" said the surprised Wolf.

"I am Jumping Mouse and I am heading up this Sacred Mountain to the top. I was wondering if you were my guide," he inquired.

"I have lost my memory and lost my way and I am of no help to anyone," said the lonely Wolf.

Mouse thought about how he'd healed Buffalo and how perhaps his eye could heal Wolf as it had Buffalo. Alas, Jumping Mouse did what he knew he had to do and offered his other eye to Brother Wolf. "Well I helped the Great Buffalo by giving him my eye and this may work to heal you as well," he said, shaking in his boots.

"Why thank you, Jumping Mouse — this is very generous of you." And before a second had passed, Jumping Mouse's remaining eye jumped clean out of its socket, into Wolf. Again Jumping Mouse was taken aback and now feeling more afraid than ever.

Suddenly, Wolf jumped up and said, "I'm a Wolf! I remember now! I'm a Wolf!" He danced up and down in delight. Taken over by his own glee, he suddenly thought about his benefactor and looked around to see a very frail mouse, totally blind and exposed.

Jumping Mouse asked Wolf, "I have to go to the top of the sacred mountain. Will you take me?"

"Of course I will. I remember the way now and it's the least I can do for such a brave soul as you," avowed Wolf.

Wolf picked up Jumping Mouse and carried him ever so carefully to the top of the mountain. It took many moons but finally they arrived at a pristine lake where Wolf gently placed Jumping Mouse down for the night. Jumping Mouse fell into darkness. He slept for days before he awoke to find himself a little disoriented but noticing that he could see ever so faintly.

As he stood up to explore where he was, he heard a loud voice exclaim, "Are you ready for the gift of medicine power?"

Jumping Mouse didn't know where the voice was coming from but answered, "Yes, yes I want medicine power."

"Then crouch down and jump as high as you possibly can."

Remembering his past experience, Jumping Mouse was a little afraid but at the same time he knew he must. He crouched down and jumped with all his might. Higher and higher he went as he grabbed hold of the wind. Suddenly, he noticed he was flying with immense wings and grace. He could see everything below him. Gliding over the mountain and down across the river, he saw brother Raccoon and Buffalo. He saw his village and the tiny weeny dots below.

He heard Magic Frog shout so loud, "Jumping Mouse you have a new name. That name is Eagle."

The End.

Mouse found courage and guidance by saying yes to his dream and not letting anything or anyone get in the way.

Okay now let's get back on track with Mice and Relationship Marketing.

<u>What you can learn from Mice:</u>

- How to see and take care of crucial details needed to get the job done.
- To see more humble aspects of oneself.
- To gather and prepare what you need to go the distance.

<u>How to enthuse Mice:</u>

- You are going to have to show great patience.
- Keep encouraging Mice to go for their dreams.
- Let Mice know you see their power and ability.

<u>If you are in the Mouse stage and ready to become Jumping Mouse, transformation is possible if:</u>

- You step out of your comfort zone, look up, and look out.
- You take a leap of faith and jump to higher ground.
- You trust the ones who went before you, to be your guides.
- You work with them and align with them.
- You learn that life is about always challenging ourselves.
- You see there's a much bigger world than the one you've been seeing.
- You take a risk to know your real self and share your mighty power.
- You serve others without keeping score.
- You really get behind other people's dreams and visions.
- You think bigger and take bolder action steps.
- You ask yourself, "Am I Mouse or Jumping Mouse?" and if you answered Jumping Mouse, then you have the ability to become Eagle.

The first time I heard the story of Jumping Mouse, I loved it and it impacted me in a powerful way. In fact, it mesmerized me in the telling. I know in many ways it is my story and I relate well to it. The thing I love about Mice is they have the greatest potential of becoming Eagles, if they are willing to lose the Mouse way of seeing.

While it may look like Mice have the furthest to go to achieving great heights, in actual fact, they are the closest; once Mice have chosen to become Jumping Mice. Mice know all the details and don't miss a beat. Mice have mastered the ground and can now come out into the light of day and be seen. Mice know how to survive. Mice know how to gather and store. It's time then to take a leap of faith and soar with the Eagles, for this is truly who you are deep down. The only way you can do this is to take risks and serve others unconditionally.

Jumping Mouse has extraordinary potential to become Eagle. Are you ready to crouch down and leap as high as you possibly can?

Chapter 14

Peacock — *Rock Star or Diva*

I want to particularly focus on this category because these individuals have what it takes to succeed in this business more than most other categories. The difficulty is, Peacocks want to apply for the senior positions in the organization. When they realize they have to begin at the beginning, as it were, they cannot quite appreciate lowering themselves to this level. Sometimes because of this initial misunderstanding about how the business works, they simply say no and walk on by.

Peacocks love to strut their stuff and why not, they are magnificently beautiful and probably very clever. They can fly as high as the local treetops but cannot soar. In general, they prefer to be close to the ground. We affectionately refer to Peacocks as Divas or Rock Stars. They love to show off their plumage and are often viewed as a symbol of pride and vanity. They easily recruit people into their endeavour but do not do so well at leading and nurturing their teams. Or they spin their wheels and have a hard time recruiting in the beginning and cannot figure out why? *The Special Ones,* is how they think of themselves in private. Peacocks are usually good presenters with some serious charisma. They have probably been successful before, in some other types of business or pursuits. They appear confident on the outside but usually this masks their vulnerability. It's hard for them to understand why they don't take off into huge success — after all don't we know who they are? They can't understand why it's not a slam-dunk for them.

Peacocks never think to join the team or ask their up-team leaders for help because they think they know best and have often alienated the very people who could help them. The reason I have affection for Peacocks is because they do have the skill base to succeed and do genuinely want to make a difference in the world — it's just that they are confused as to how this business works. It is vastly different from most other work environments and cultures. Unlike other business structures, in Relationship Marketing, we are empowered to work together and give real support to people in our teams. This is not just a nice altruistic idea. How many CEOs out there are working towards promoting you into their positions? None or very few are. And why would they, when only one position is available? But in Relationship Marketing this is the name of the game. And it's not about what you can do yourself but what you can duplicate. (You'll hear me say this many times throughout this book.) Peacocks are great at that initial stage of imparting their knowledge and dazzling people. The gap is in duplicating their skills and helping those people to build their businesses. It takes time to lead, nurture, and grow your team and this is Peacock's weakness.

Peacocks are not very coachable because they are not willing to give up control and unfortunately fall short of the mark they intend for themselves. Some success may occur in the beginning but not as fast or with as much fame as they were expecting. Astonished, they work harder, pride still intact, until finally, indignant, they find fault with you or the company and strut away before anyone notices. (Or so they think.)

So first, Peacocks have to learn how to take responsibility for the team they are creating. Having a power of influence is a responsibility in itself and if we influence and invite someone to join our team, we need to make sure we support and connect him or her to the support infrastructure appropriately.

Please, if you recognize yourself, we really want you to stay and share your talents with the team and the company.

<u>What you can learn from Peacocks:</u>

- Their talent of attraction. — What specifically are they doing?
- To adopt a little of the Peacock's confidence and swagger.
- Their skill base, to be creative and communicate well.

<u>How to enthuse Peacocks:</u>

- Encourage them to take responsibility for the people they are bringing into the business. It's not about recruiting and moving on.
- Offer them a leadership role as quickly as possible.
- Make sure you know their 'why' and reason to excel as specifically as you can.
- Let them know how important they are to the Company and Team.
- Recognize their skills, experience, and talent, and show them how to recognize and celebrate others.
- Help them to see the benefits and potential gained by stepping through the initiating process that comes with Relationship Marketing.

<u>If you are in the Peacock stage and now ready to fly, transformation is possible if:</u>

- You are willing to sit in the passenger seat and let yourself be shown the way by the ones who are already succeeding. Stay in the passenger seat until you are forced into the driver's seat — not when you say so but when the game puts you there.
- You become humble, open, and coachable.
- You become a leader rather than a recruiter and also a good follower.

- You edify and honour others on your team. It's not about you.
- You hone your ability to hold the space for others and see and know what is needed for the game to move. Inclusiveness is highly important here.
- You duplicate yourself by showing others how to do what you do.
- You let go of competition and move into co-operation with others.
- You connect your new people with the team, hold hands, and do not let go.

Peacocks can become Eagles or Dolphins, if they first recognize their dilemma and learn from it.

Many times I have found myself as the Peacock, thinking I'm so great and have got it all together. In the beginning, I was a great recruiter but not a great leader. I had to learn how to lead, follow through, and develop a skill base with which I had no previous experience. Stepping in and moving forward in this business was, for me, the beginning of a slippery slope that catapulted me into a rapid professional development program. I had never run a successful business before and was not very good at using systems. I was negligent, mostly from a lack of experience in how to lead my growing team. In the beginning, I resisted many aspects that I later understood to be important and essential. I was asked to lead and didn't realize at the time how I was holding my own team back by my lack of skill and experience. Fortunately though, I did one thing really well and that was to work with a brilliant mentor who had all of these skills in spades. It is why it is the best business in the world. In the beginning, you don't have to be the expert. Simply hold hands with your up team leaders and learn on the job.

I have had several peacocks enter my business and then leave or get stuck. In many ways, I feel sad for them because they are suited for this business and definitely have the skill base. They are often holders of big visions and need the kind of support available with this business system. If they are willing to humble themselves and integrate with the bigger team, this vehicle could be excellent for them to shine, big time.

Chapter 15

Shark — *Caution*

Sharks are rare visitors and I hope you never experience one on your team. They are usually serial MLM/Network Marketers, looking for the best opportunity at any cost. Unlike Eagles, who may also be professional Network Marketers, they do not have any loyalty to your company or team and are capable of doing some serious damage. BE CAREFUL — because they have their own type of charisma and are masters at courting you.

Sharks usually enter through the back door; getting a head start by buying their way into a higher position. Or in many cases, Sharks have been lured away to join another company. Sharks have the power of influence and such strong conviction that when they say jump, their team of followers says: How high and where are we going next? They build extraordinarily fast and you wouldn't want to get in their way.

Sharks are baiters, with strong egos and powerful personalities. They are masters at manipulation and in it for what they can devour. To them you are nothing but meat caught in their trap. There is zero loyalty or heart and if you are sensitive you will notice Sharks right away.

They are able to create big success while they are with you. However if the company falters and goes through a difficult phase, which invariably happens, especially with start up companies, they pick up their teams and leave. As the relationship was never based on loyalty, they do not stay. They do not lobby for change within the company nor do they take a stand. Instead, they up and leave all together and it can be shocking to the company and the field when they exit *en masse*. I hope this never happens to you but it could, which is why I am bringing it to your attention.

I have experienced several of them in this business (luckily not in my team) and at first I was convinced they cared and wanted to make a real difference in the world. I found out abruptly, when they left, that they had no ability for compassion or interest in anyone else but themselves. It's not their fault; it's just the nature of the beast they have become. They may have been battered, bruised, and bashed around by life, which may have given them their sharp edges. Watch out for them.

Every now and again (but this is rare), Shark stay and then move up into another stage and begin sincerely to build their business. Sometimes you can swim with a shark but you need to be discerning and be very, very careful.

Do not fall victim to Sharks. Remain empowered and aware and send only good thoughts in their direction.

It's part of the polarity of life and if you are awake you can even learn from them. It's not that what they teach isn't good and beneficial; it's more about who they are behind their disguises. Just be careful not to get stung, bitten or led astray. Stay awake in their presence. Since Sharks are visitors only, I have not included them in the Tribe photo.

Chapter 16

Sheep — *Sheepish*

Sheep are timid, nervous, and easily frightened. Held back by their defencelessness, they have a tough time trusting. It would take a great deal of courage for them to be able to step out in a big way. Sometimes they achieve a certain level of success but will find a ceiling and get stuck there. Sheep, by nature, are followers; they tend to lack independent thought, are not very ambitious and feel vulnerable when left alone. They are content to be in the middle of it all rather than to be leading. Maybe they have been wounded and as a result tend to focus on what could go wrong again and choose to play it safe. Maybe they have had a lot of disappointment from their efforts in the past and don't want to trust again. They have good reason to feel afraid and in order to support them, you have to help them to feel safe, which can take a great deal of patience but is definitely well worthwhile. They are also compassionate, kind, genuine, and affectionate so treat them with great respect please.

Sheep suffer from a lack of self-confidence and must have a leader (shepherd) to rely on to feel secure. If they fall down, they cannot get up by themselves so you have to go and help them get up. They are often creatures of habit and get in ruts easily, sadly not ever really knowing their true gifts and talents. Reach out to them often because it's all about timing and it may be time for them to shine. Ultimately, until they are tired of being afraid and hiding behind the flock, they are unable to help themselves to really be successful.

It's not that you need to give up on them — quite the contrary. It's just that when you are moving forward in your business, you need to attract strong leaders who are open to growth every step of the way, with a sense of urgency. Every level brings a new set of obstacles or challenges and sometimes Sheep will not go the distance with you. But when Sheep do come out to play, grow, and succeed — just like Care Bear, there is a huge celebration in store and much delight. How you can help them is to be their shepherd and lead them into their fullest expression, if they are willing. If they are not willing or able, then just love them anyway. They are still important members of your team. Be mindful always that achieving a promotion and monetary success is not the name of the game for everyone. Sometimes Sheep move into a Tortoise phase (customer) and sometimes they move up to one of the other phases with some training, commitment, and courage. Either way, it's perfect so you don't have to sweat it.

<u>What you can learn from Sheep:</u>

- How to find and learn from a great shepherd (mentor).
- How to be sensitive to danger in the field (Shark).
- To be humble and follow along with the flock when you need to.
- That there is strength in numbers.

<u>How to enthuse Sheep:</u>

- Go and find them if they retreat.
- Give them your attention and support.
- Pick them up if they're down and give them encouragement.

If you are in the Sheep stage, transformation is possible if:

- You let go of past disappointments and experiences, get into present-day reality, and look at the possibilities right in front of you.
- You stop sheep walking and find out what is unique about you.
- You are brave and share your talents.
- You're willing to build your confidence and move out of your comfort zone.
- You find a good shepherd to support you and help build your flock.
- You focus outwards on other people. When we serve others, we forget about our own problems.
- You learn to be bold and brave no matter what it feels like. Leadership courses would help you through this.
- You ultimately step up to the plate as the shepherd/leader.
- You step forward to the next level with courage and share your gifts and talents.

Can I relate to Sheep? Not so much since joining this business but definitely prior to it. I have spent many a day, week, month and even years as the Sheep, where I was afraid of stepping out. I didn't want to speak up and lead even though I felt an inner call urging me forward. My flock was my home, couch, TV, and pets. I encourage you to do whatever it takes to step forward because what you say and who you are is important and your soul needs you to. Remember this is simply a pattern or stage and one you can transform out of…Are you ready?

Chapter 17

Skunk — *Reputation*

Skunk do not threaten your life but they can threaten your senses.

We all broadcast a certain kind of brand or frequency and it either resonates or does nothing, or it can even repel people. In the case of Skunk, they are preceded by their reputations and people will be cautious around them.

Skunk are strong energy. In leaking vital energy, they may be stinking up the environment without realizing it. Usually this is because Skunk comes across as pushy or intrusive salesmen, possibly downloading their sales pitch or personal agenda on an unsuspecting person with whom they have not yet made a connection. Sometimes there is a disconnect between what they think is happening and what is actually happening in the environment.

Skunk certainly mean well and try very hard but when they start spraying their expertise all over you, people run in the opposite direction. There is a real innocence here because often Skunk are unaware that people are already on guard around them. They could have some great candidates for their business but tend to push potential partners away within a short period of time by this unconsciousness. If Skunk's self-esteem isn't high they may smell up the area by trying too hard to be friendly and kind. Therefore they come across as a little intense.

I have witnessed Skunk walk into a crowd and try to join, and within a few minutes, the crowd dissipates and they're not sure why. They're really well intentioned but clumsy with compromised vision and poor social skills. They're not aware that they have not yet made a connection when they meet someone because they are not present to see or feel it. People want to know that you care before they open up to you and trust what you have to offer. How can you show that you care? Listening of course and witnessing the other, is the key that unlocks treasures.

Skunks carry a strong obnoxious scent as a defence and they have good reason for this in the wild. This safety mechanism of repelling is beneficial in nature, however, in this business, it is about attracting rather than repelling. Knowing they are not alone and are part of the Tribe, and holding hands with others makes Skunk more comfortable and less reliant on acknowledgement for their expertise.

I love watching my Skunks wake up to this and grow quickly into the next phase. They are open to feedback and want to do well, so the transformation you can witness in them is pretty special.

What you can learn from Skunk:

- How to be selective with who you work with.
- Skunks knowledge is vast and they love to share what they know.
- How to set boundaries.
- How to dig deep burrows and find out where the jewels are hidden.

How to enthuse Skunk:

- Let your Skunk know you care. Be genuine.
- Hold hands and be the partner that they need to support them.
- Be patient and let them know you will not go away.
- Listen to their stories.
- Be firm with them and do not put up with skunky behaviour. (They actually appreciate this).

<u>If you are in the Skunk stage, transformation is possible if:</u>

- You learn when you are in rapport and when you are not.
- You trust the reputation of respect you carry.
- You ask people: What do you think? And then have the grace to listen.
- You STOP trying to sell — this is not a convincing business.
- You watch out for dumping all of your woes on anyone who will listen.
- You relax, no need to push. Become *present*. Breathe.
- You learn to love yourself. You really are loveable....
- You build a relationship first and make the connection by listening and finding out about the person and what makes them tick.
- You become comfortable with silent spaces — you don't have to fill them in or be on-guard.
- You respect other people's space.

I have been guilty of this skunky behaviour on occasion and it was because I was feeling inept and out of place. Or else it was because I was so certain my great business opportunity was right for someone, who was not interested. As I have grown to trust myself and become my own best friend, it rarely happens, as I'm no longer caught up in trying to prove something. Also, as I have confidence in my company and what I have to offer, I no longer need to convince anyone. I trust the resonance of how this business moves.

I think it boils down to self-acceptance. When we love and accept ourselves, people pick up on this and we are more pleasant to be around.

Remember this is more than a business; instead you are embarking on a journey of profound professional and personal transformation. See if you can find a much bigger picture in what you are offering. And remember: Find out first what the other person needs before offering your opportunity. You are listening to them to find out if they are looking for a solution and also if they are ready now to change. You may or may not have the right fit for them. This is what you have to discover. At the very least you may find a new friend.

Chapter 18

Tortoise — *Our Customers*

Slow and steady is the name of the game. They are our loyal customers with a huge lifespan, (you hope). They absolutely love the products, respect the company, and are very much a part of what you are doing, even if it is silently. They're not interested in running with any pack or going on any incentive trip but are happy and content doing their thing. They bring delight to your team whenever they do show up at an event (and sometimes they do). Otherwise they sit in the backdrop of your business. No real transformation is necessary unless they choose one day to get involved in the business, in which case they become subject to the same opportunity for personal and professional development as everyone else. Otherwise our job is simply to understand them and appreciate their constant presence in our business.

How to enthuse Tortoise:

- Support them to share their story.
- Bring them to the community.
- Watch how their interaction with others makes a difference.
- Invite them back if their account has lapsed.
- Ask them who they know who would like to know about your products or services.
- Show them how they can make a difference in other people's lives.
- Show rewards for their referrals.

It's important to remember they love a phone call from time to time, so make sure you check in with them and thank them for their loyalty. Be truly grateful for these precious members because they may make upwards of 80% of your business.

Chapter 19

Summarizing Part One

Do you recognize yourself? Do you recognize members of your Team? You may find yourself a little in one category and a little in another — this is possible and probable. As we become aware and transform it's like morphing from one to another. The question is: **Are you willing and ready to transform your position, if need be?**

What I notice now is, as soon as I become aware of where I am stuck, it changes. Awareness is the key. We cannot change what we do not acknowledge, so begin by asking yourself the truth about your business and the results you are getting.

What I love about the Tribe is that together, the whole becomes a beautiful tapestry of different colours and textures. This collage is more fun and engaging than if the entire Tribe were comprised of one particular group. All of the different characteristics and phases evolve towards becoming our highest and best and why not? After all, it is all just a mind-set and today in this profession, people are becoming more and more authentic and open to being spontaneous and real.

If you were to dismantle a Swiss clock and place all the parts on a table, you would see many, many parts. Every single part has a role to play and without the; coils, rivets, spirals, washers, nuts, springs, bolts, pins, wires, clicks, hooks, rings, and other assortments, this clock could not work. When you, or the clock maker, put it all back together again, it will run with pure precision. Your Tribe is made up of authentic characters, coming together for an individual and common purpose. I love what Dr. Deepak Chopra says about this; "The universe has no spare parts."

The precision of the team is a work of art. Your Tribe cannot function as well without you playing your part.

So…

- What part are you playing?
- Know that your part is important; never doubt the role you play.
- What are your strengths?
- Who are you? Find out what makes you tick.
- What gifts and talents are you bringing to the team?
- How does this all work together?

There is a direct correlation between your personal development experience and the success of your business. Remember it can be a Self-Actualizing program with a compensation plan, so have patience with yourself and with the members of your team. I have had members of my team disappear for literally years and return, seemingly out of the blue; renewed and transformed. I absolutely love this about this business and it's truly fulfilling to see the transformation taking place, in and all around me. My passion is to witness the unseen potential and activate it into reality. Have fun with this and don't take it personally. Remember, these categories are not pointing at who you are but at what phase of business you may be in and are intended to show how to move forward, if necessary, and if you want to.

I want to be perfectly clear that I'm not suggesting you are a Beaver or you are a Mouse etc. but more that you may be showing up in this characteristic or stage of your journey.

You may have within you the essence of that animal that you can relate to, learn from, and give as a gift. Maybe you didn't know you had that gift to give but it is part of your true nature. That is the motive behind this book. Many people ask me what animal they are. And I say, "I'm not answering that question. You answer that question yourself by reading through and looking at the characteristics you most relate to. And it will change along the way and you will watch it and witness change with the people in your Tribe."

PART TWO —
How to Work Effectively with Your Tribe

Chapter 20

Issues that Hold People Back

I like to believe anybody can do this business but the truth is, it's not for everyone. Of those who are called, only a few excel in this business — why is that?

I would say anybody can earn enough money in the profession to get their products paid for and since there are some outstanding products on the market today, this will attract many, many people. Others may enjoy a steady $400-$500 extra each month to supplement their income and they will be ecstatic. This is fully achievable by the masses.

This book is for the ones who want to *go all the way* and are willing and ready to do the work — not only the work of the business but studying the profession and really tuning into your Tribe. In these next chapters, I have shared some of what I consider the most important and relevant ways of doing this. As you study *From Squeak to Roar* and learn the characteristics and phases of your Relationship Marketing Tribe, you will learn what it takes to not only survive but also to thrive in this profession.

I have found the only difference between a person struggling in this business and a person with a successful, sustainable business is their **intention** and the degree of **fear or love** they carry within. Let me explain what I mean by this.

   a. Intention is something we tune into and this tuning-in aspect is what I want to highlight here. You see we think we have control over everything and that maybe by setting strong goals and then taking all the right actions — our plan will manifest. Sometimes you will take all the right actions and nothing happens. How frustrating is that? But upon deeper investigation you can probably uncover what really wants to happen that perhaps is more apropos.

I love it when I tune into what wants to happen in my life rather than trying to force it. It's a bit like my will versus Thy will. Thy will always outperforms my will when I trust enough to follow along with it even when it feels unknown. A clue is that it begins with a desire or an inspiration. In this business, our reason Why we are engaged in it is such an important focus that will keep us moving forward and buoyant when we feel like giving up.

b. You can do this business with love (open hearted, caring for others) or you can do it with fear (closed, brakes on, manipulative), and based on this you will find totally different results. The most important influence is that of connecting to people and their dreams, helping people to get free and building supportive relationships.

It takes a certain kind of mind-set or attitude to succeed and here are some of the patterns I have found that stop people from achieving what they say they want. Assuming, of course, they have the other side of the equation in place, which is: great company, great products, team, corporate support, vision, and resources.

1. They have not yet made the decision/commitment to do this business. Not ALL IN. You have to want it so bad that the action required is of no consequence.

2. They are not connected to a leader or plugged in to the overall team and are going it alone (Lone Wolf).

3. They don't have the strategies or systems to support their business i.e. Business Plan, Method of Operation, phone plan, Internet, investment to travel if needed, etc.

4. They lack passion

5. They have not connected what they are doing to a higher purpose.

6. They do not relate or align the business with their bigger vision. (Similar as above but different)

7. FEAR — (Deer, Sheep, Mice). They are afraid of:
   - rejection
   - being criticized
   - failing
   - succeeding
   - a myriad of other reasons
   - what other people will think

8. They are not hungry enough for change and prefer their comfort zone (Cat, Tortoise).

9. They are caught in an instinctive pattern.[4]

10. They are not open to the growth that is forced upon them if they step towards success.

11. They are not aware yet of what they're *really* doing, i.e. they're skunking on people by flogging products or spraying their expertise.

12. They lack personal accountability and consistency (Hare).

13. They are lazy — not willing to do the work (Cat).

14. Their level of belief about being financially free is too low.

15. They don't believe in themselves therefore people will not follow them. If people do not believe the messenger, they will not believe the message.

16. They are not open to the personal development side of the business.

---

4   Meney, Elinor. www.instinx.com

17. They give up too soon (Hare) or follow the wrong people (Shark).

18. They are not a product of the products. (You have to be loyal and take your company's products).

19. They think it's a *get rich quick scheme* and with entitlement issues intact — expecting it to just happen.

Or perhaps it truly is not their path and they need to let go and move on.

One of the things that you really need in order to move forward in this business is an unstoppable belief; a solid belief in what you're doing and with whom you're doing it. If you have a strong leader with confidence, who can show you the ropes, you too will have more certainty stepping forward. After all, who wants to follow a person across a wobbly bridge? That is why if you are new and you are building your baby team, make sure to connect them with your up team as soon as possible. Your job is to be a connector to where the confidence and credibility is. Note: Not all 'up-team' sponsors have this posture and you may have to look further a field.

A quick example I'd like to share with you: I was out riding one day with my friend Richard. He too grew up in England and on the back of a horse. I knew he was a crazy good rider and we always had great adventures out on the trail. This one-day, we were heading towards the lake when we saw a fairly big tree had fallen across our path. Stopped for a moment to contemplate the situation, I thought, there is no way we're going over that. Richard, however, had a different plan. Before I could say anything, he was off his horse, handed me the reins and started kicking off the protruding branches around the tree. OMG it looked like he was actually going to jump the tree. (I hadn't jumped since a teenager). Sure enough, he came over, grabbed the reins, jumped back on his horse and said, "Let's go." Before I had time to think about it and worry too much, I was on the other side of the tree. It was exhilarating and we ended up having a great ride. I thought about this afterwards and how easy it was for me to follow him in spite of my original reaction. By myself I would have turned back. Not only did he have confidence in his own ability, he had confidence in mine.

In this business, you have to find someone who is holding out a solid ground for you; a leader who engenders an environment of confidence; one who shows you how to go over or around obstacles; a person who doesn't just show you the way but does it with you. I was fortunate to have a leader like this when I first started in this business. I literally had no idea what I was doing, yet was succeeding rapidly in the first few months. And that is the beauty of this business. I got to borrow her confidence and knowledge until I learned the ropes. In other words, you learn on the job, versus having to learn the job before you can begin.

Here are some important guidelines that can turn around the issues that may have held you back and will help you move forward into success:

1. Make the Decision. Commit to it and BE ALL IN. (Even if that is part-time. Whatever time you have towards it, be ALL IN.)

2. Find a great leader to help you (Eagle, Dolphin, Dog, Beaver, Lynx).

3. Make sure you're plugged in to the overall team. It really is a team sport. If you find yourself being the Lone Wolf, notice it and change it by connecting right away to the people who can support you. Remember you are instinctively a pack animal.

4. Make sure you have the systems and strategies needed to build a successful, sustainable business. (Beaver can teach you.) Be coachable in other words.

5. Get over thinking it is a *get rich quick* scheme — it most certainly is not. Find the right company, find your Tribe and jump

in with all fours or twos, for at least five years. Watch out for Hare tendencies of running away, especially when you start to achieve some success.

6. Connect what you are doing to the action of service and paying it forward. Your contribution offers a higher purpose to something far greater than simply selling products and earning a living.

7. Align it to a bigger vision and bring your passion by sharing your gifts and talents. This passion is like a laser beam helping you to move fast towards success.

8. Watch out for FEAR: rejection, being criticized, failing, succeeding, or concern about what people will think, (get over this one right away if you can). *Fear is an illusion. Watch it and it disappears.*

9. Get used to being uncomfortable. If you are willing to get out of your comfort zone on a daily basis, you are sure to grow your business and grow yourself. All it takes is courage.

10. Be open to the growth that will certainly happen as you step forward towards success. (You may have to change some attitudes and let go of some old stories you may be running).

11. Do not hold the posture of: *I have to flog my products on you.* People hate being sold to. Respect the intelligence of your potential partners and learn how to do this business consciously and authentically. If you have a great product and a great company, be confident because you have the main ingredients. The rest has to do with you and your readiness to change. Are you ready? Find a problem your potential partner or customer may have and see if what you have to offer is a solution. First rule: Meet people where they are.

12. CONSISTENCY is major in this business. It can make or break you. This means being dependable so that your team

can rely on you. Your team does what you do, so consistently show up for work.

13. Don't just change the way you think, change the way you talk. Be mindful what you are saying to yourself and to others. Listen and become aware of your language. What are you saying?

14. SHOW UP and be ACCOUNTABLE for your actions and your business. Treat it like a business and not a hobby.

15. If you catch yourself with an excuse (any excuse) bust yourself right away. You are the one with the power — do not give it away by blaming.

16. Be sure to have fun. People will be attracted to having fun and then it never feels like work (Dolphin, Dog).

17. Allow yourself to develop your intuitive side of this business (Lynx, Horse).

18. Find your passion — it is the driving force to your dreams.

Our world is our mirror. See what you can learn from the people showing up around you.

Chapter 21

How to Warm Up a Cold Market

If you have never heard the term, cold market, then great; you will not need this reframing exercise. But you may find someone joining your team for whom this term looms heavy. So what is a cold market? The cold market refers to strangers and people we haven't met yet. Warm market would be people who know us by first name, for example; family, friends, colleagues, dentist, hair stylist, dog walker, landlord...etc. You get the idea.

I built my business with a warm market but I know people who have built their very successful businesses with a completely cold market. Success can happen either way and some people prefer to approach people they do not know. Let's begin by taking the pressure off the term 'cold market.' It is unappealing and impersonal. I prefer *potential market* and think of it as friends we haven't met yet. Instead of referring to people as *prospects*, I love Michael Oliver's term, *potential partners*.[5] Doesn't that feel warmer already?

While we are on the subject, I like to refer to people in the business as *associates* rather than *distributors*, for two reasons. First, it is not an accurate description of what we do, as the company does the distributing. We, the associates, connect people to the company as customers or associates and train, educate and work along side them. Second, the term *associates* is friendlier and more engaging.

---

5   Oliver, Michael. How to Sell Network Marketing Without Fear, Anxiety or Losing your Friends! Natural Selling Inc. 2002

How to Connect with Potential Partners

This is not a business of convincing; it is a business of caring and connecting. You will succeed and succeed rapidly with your *potential market* if you remember that. Wayne Dyer[6] says it best when he says *People don't care how much you know until they know how much you care.* It's amazing what a smile and a warm hello can do.

If you can master giving your full, aware attention to a person, you will make an impact on him or her. Our job is not to sell to someone as much as it is to simply sound our tuning fork and see who rises up to the occasion. Imagine being in someone's presence who is empty of agenda and he or she is giving you complete undivided attention. You can tell by the eye contact and how he or she is listening to you. I'm sure you have witnessed this in your life. How did it feel? You probably felt important and heard. This is quite rare and it is the mastery I speak of. It is the beginning of creating warmth in a cold market. Practice with everyone you come in contact with. If for no other reason, you will have made a difference in someone else's life. I think most people could use a really good listening to, don't you?

It's just an illusion that we are separate from each other and if you pay close attention, you will start to notice what the other person is thinking. If you pay really close attention and look at the body language and into the eyes of the other person, you start to know the soul of that person. When connecting at this deeper level, you start to become warm and available very fast. This can happen without sales scripts or jargon and with very few words. It's all about the energy you stand in, otherwise known as posture.

When you claim such mastery, you have to be impeccable with all interactions because people will know whether you are genuine or not. You cannot manufacture authenticity; you cannot pretend to care. It is either there or it isn't.

6   Dyer, Wayne. www.drwaynedyer.com

Once you meet someone you think you would like as a friend or potential partner, begin building the relationship. We usually know very quickly when we meet a person if we like him or her. However it may take a little longer to find out if that person is suitable and has a need that our business venture may fulfill.

Here's a little recap to make that connection:

- Smile and say hello.
- Be open and relax.
- Give your undivided attention.
- Listen to what the person is saying.
- Ask questions to open the connection (not too many).
- Feel your body and notice your breathing (helps you become present).
- Focus on the person, not what's going on around you.
- If you notice thoughts, agendas, or shopping lists taking space, bring yourself back.
- Wake up and reconnect.
- Open your heart and pay attention to subtle cues.
- Be unattached to the outcome.

How and Where to Find Potential Partners

Discovering potential partners begins with your clear intention and the criteria of common values you want to attract in a person. It is literally about finding new friends. Finding friends seems to be easier the younger we are but why not adopt a consciousness and clear decision to open to this at every age?

Is it that some of us find it easier to meet friends; as in the case of Dog, Horse, Dolphin, Deer, and Mice, or is it a learned ability? I think anyone can choose to be friendly and kind.

As you put yourself out there, you make yourself available to Divine connections, as I call them. Simply stay open to all possibilities and keep your feelers out. It is important to pay attention to your intuition. When you have an impulse to go somewhere, go. Go...don't argue with where you have to go. Sometimes you get the thought to go to the grocery store and you say, *I don't need anything at the grocery store.* Well go anyway because that may be the coincidence about to happen, if you let it.

When we go to a networking event, we all know why we're there. It feels a little phony and somewhat fake at times but you can be the one who's different. You can be the one making meaningful connections. Rather than giving out your business cards and propaganda, receive *potential partners'* business cards instead. Enjoy the experience of the moment with each conversation you have. Pay attention to who is in the room and ask yourself the question: Is there anyone in this room who is willing and ready to join me? Allow the grace of connection to introduce you. Relax, because there are so many people ready for what you have to offer — just don't offer it right away. Simply begin the conversation and when you work with the principles mentioned above, you can trust yourself to be naturally guided into the next right question or response. No need to sweat it. Don't worry about verbiage; remember you cannot say the wrong thing to the right person and vice versa. (Occasionally it does happen if you are being pushy or skunky).

The magic will unfold when you allow the game to come to you more. Trust the process and have more fun with it because people really pick up on a more light-hearted approach.

There are so many different ways to meet people and widen your circle. Here are a few suggestions:

- Social Media. On-line with Linked In, Facebook, Twitter, Webinars, Google+, etc.

- At Starbucks or other coffee shops, the library, a club, the gym, skiing, etc...You name it.
- Sports activities.
- Conventions or retreats.
- Neighborhood events and groups.
- Walking your dog in the dog park.
- Take a class, or go to a lecture.
- Forums, chat rooms and other social media sites of interest to you.
- Music events.
- Creating YouTube Videos.
- Websites and blogs.
- Business networking and Meetup.com.
- Volunteering.

I used to have a bad attitude about on-line, social media-type connections. I judged them as awkward and inauthentic. I don't know what I was thinking because it is totally possible to be organically drawn to some great potential partners this way. Especially when you move into global markets. We have awesome ways of virtually connecting to people all over the world — let alone in the next town.

Wherever you are going and whatever you are doing, Relationship Marketing can simply wrap around your life in a natural and fun way. For example; getting your nails or hair done, walking around the park, in the line-up at the grocery store, or on an airplane.

Here's a great example: Out riding with my daughter one day, we were almost at the end of the ride when we decided to go a little farther. As we headed off down the road, I got this feeling that we should go back. The message was very clear and strong and I said to my daughter, "I think we should turn around and go back," — though I didn't know why.

Right away she looked at me and said, "Mum I got the same feeling. That's weird."

So without further ado, we turned our horses around and headed back home. Just as we were approaching the barn, I saw a lovely young couple wandering down the road.

We said hello and briefly connected while I was still on my horse. I asked them how long they were staying and what was the special occasion for their visit. They responded, "We're taking a few days off work because we feel underappreciated in our jobs and we are here to think about what kind of business we could create together."

Can you imagine how badly I wanted to blurt out that I had the perfect opportunity for them? Instead, we chatted for a while and I asked them all about themselves, while I was un-tacking my horse. Within minutes there was warmth between us that was undeniable. The apparent cold market became warm within minutes by our connection. I never mentioned what I had to offer at all but invited them for tea the following day.

So once again, here are the steps I took:

- I followed my intuition by turning my horse around and going back, so that I could line up with them by Divine appointment. (I may never have met them otherwise).
- I got into rapport with them.
- I created the curiosity.
- I didn't let the cat out of the bag too soon.

As a result, I now have this adorable couple in my business and new friends in my life.

When to Hang in and When to Let Go of Potential Partners

There is no need to convince or beg anybody. Relax and listen to the truth being spoken. I heard one of the pros in the industry say that it might take eight to twelve exposures before a person joins you. So know when to persevere and when to let go.

You may even find that the *potential market* is warmer than your warm market. Those friends you have been trying to get into your business for years can cause you the biggest grief, if you're attached to them joining you. I have friends I would love to have joined me in my business. When the tuning fork rang they didn't hear it. They didn't relate to the resonating tone and therefore it wasn't a fit.

You don't want to burn out your friends and family and further perpetuate the story of losing friends in this industry. And for those it isn't appropriate for, please do everybody a favour, and don't harass them. Be professional. There are so many great companies out there and everyone will find the one that fits them, if they are sincerely looking. They will find the one where they too will feel the; *yes this is the one; yes this is my company; yes this is my tribe; yes this is my mission, and yes this is my movement.* By freeing them to find their right company, you are freeing yourself at the same time.

On the other hand, you have to know when to stay with people and not give up on them. As I mentioned, the person who invited me into the business, invited me to an event six times and each time I turned her down and was not very friendly. She didn't give up on me though because she knew what I didn't know and was willing to put her credibility on the line for me. Thank God she didn't give up. Until you fully realize what you have in your hands, you may be negatively affected by the attitudes of unaware people. I was one of them (unaware that is). If you are a person who gets discouraged easily by what other people think, you may find this business hard until you fully appreciate the gift you have in your hands. The opportunity here is getting over what people think of you. For this alone it is an endeavour worth embarking upon.

Since it took several attempts to get me to say *yes*, I now have that direct experience as a useful reminder. And because of this, the odd time I will go after a person. Not with my agenda or pitch but with my transparency and heart. I will put my credibility on the line for certain people, if I really feel this would be perfect for them and I can tell they just don't know what they don't know. And providing of course they eventually hear the tuning fork. It is a fine line and a subtle distinction to know the difference between hanging in and letting go. Be mindful.

Remember:

- No begging or pleading.
- Trust your intuition and respond accordingly
- Your potential market may be warmer than your warm market.
- Don't burn out friends or harass people.
- Be professional.
- Know when to hold and when to fold.

Chapter 22

Journey from Willingness to Readiness

Willingness and Readiness are two different attitudes — One you can control, the other seems to be under the jurisdiction of some cosmic agenda.

If we are evaluating whether people are ripe to join your business, it's important to get a picture of where they are in their lives and how willing and ready they are to make a big change. Also you may have members of your team who say they want to go up to the next level in their business, the question is; are they ready?

Has a potential partner ever told you, that they really do want to succeed and that they are ready? Yet in your heart of hearts, you know they are only using the words and are unaware of their inner states. They are not telling you or themselves the truth. Unfortunately what people say and what they mean are often incongruent. Eventually the results speak louder than words and often disappointment or disillusionment ensues. Notice also where you yourself think you are in regards to your own business. Have you told yourself the truth? How well do you know yourself? Do you really want what you say you want?

Here are the Four Levels you will encounter along the way:

Level 1: (Toe in) Moderately Interested.

"A nice idea," or "I think I would like that one day," — (still in the future). Doing Relationship Marketing and building a team is in the head as a concept. Maybe it's someone else's idea not yours. You still like your comfort zone a little too much and are truly nowhere near ready to move forward. You're not in enough discomfort or pain to motivate change, but are still kind of interested though not emotionally connected to the business. People may have little or no awareness of the full potential being offered. If you join at this level and begin, chances of success are very slim. You probably will stop at the first hiccup because you are not committed — perhaps only with your toe.

For those considering whether these potential tribe members qualify as ready to take a full dip — ask questions. If you pay really close attention you will hear their response right away. Tell yourself the truth before you spend hours, days, weeks and hundreds of dollars trying to make them ready. If, after exposing them to the community and products etc., they are not leaning forward to the deep end, it probably isn't the right time for them.

Level 2: (Head and toe in) Willingness with some effort.

There is more awareness of your life circumstances needing to change. You may be intellectually aware but still not emotionally aware. Maybe you're feeling a real need to change your situation but still haven't bought into any particular action steps for your problem. Your resolve is stronger and the "willingness" is amped up a little but no decision has been made yet. Some success may happen but again, it is not real unless you get to true **readiness**.

Level 3: (Head, heart and most of your body) Really willing.

You have the attitude of: *Tell me, show me what to do and I'll do it.* **You are** persistent and are letting the universe know this is your true intention. You are engaged in the process and taking necessary action no matter how difficult. You show up with commitment. You're clear about why you are doing the business. There is a deepening of your *why*. You have endurance and you are deliberate in your actions. This is a delicate stage because sometimes you feel you are being tested and you want to quit. You are doing all the right things, working hard, but still not excelling the way you would like. You're on the precipice of change though. So don't give up. At this point, taking consistent small steps can yield huge results and more importantly move you into Level 4.

Then seemingly out of nowhere the decision gets made. Some people refer to it as surrender or in a sense, handing their situation over. Then one day, voilà...readiness has arrived.

Level 4: (Full body, heart, head and soul engaged) READY.

100% on board, a full-on YES. Here you experience a complete alignment of the head, heart, and soul. The decision has been made. You may be absolutely sick and tired of the old ways and will do whatever is needed now to change. You know what you want and are emotionally involved. All excuses go out the window. The effort factor is of no consequence because in your mind-set it's virtually a done deal and you will do whatever it takes. You're no longer attached to any old story. It's the end of the old contract. You feel a complete congruency with your thoughts, actions, and results. Where before it seemed so difficult, suddenly grace and ease take over and you are living in the sweet spot. There is still a challenge but a feeling of excitement comes with it. A quiet knowing that you are on track is present and all is unfolding perfectly.

Readiness (Level 4) is part of the great mystery and no amount of pushing, praying, or begging can move it or bring it about. I've always said if we could bottle 'readiness' and sell it, we would be billionaires pretty quick. However, we can use it as a gauge to determine where a potential partner is coming from or with your team members who say they want to advance to the next levels.

Are they ready and willing? Or just willing? It saves us so much time and energy if we can see people and meet them where they are. It's not about right or wrong/good or bad, it's the present stage mind-set that prepares for what's next.

Remember also the 80/20 rule (20% of the people do 80% of the work) and that not everyone is going to want to really go for it. Most people in your business will be customers or people earning less than $500 per month. (Read about Tortoise.) It is because not everyone wants to do this as a primary business. Many prefer it to be a hobby or side business to supplement their income or to get their products paid for. At least if you know what a person's intentions are, and more importantly what their commitments are, you can relax and move with the ones who are ready to move now. Find your A Team in the 20%. They will go the distance with you and likely will resonate as your Tribe.

I would treat people in Level 3 with as much importance and commitment as Level 4 because they really are on the edge and close to the point of reaching for their dreams. I would give lots of time and focus to this Level because they are putting in the effort and not hiding in excuses.

Here is an example to help you understand this:

I met with a member of my team who I didn't know very well, since he was several levels deep in my organization. He had asked me to help him with the business, so I sat down and listened to his situation. Even though he had been involved in the business for about a year, he hadn't achieved any success and didn't know if he still wanted to be involved in it. He felt embarrassed talking to people about the company and couldn't imagine being successful.

I asked him what he wanted. He didn't know. He said he had made the commitment to do the business twice, but nothing much was happening. He said he was disappointed when the people he thought would love to work with him, didn't want to.

I asked him again, "What do you want?"

He said, "To make a lot of money. I thought it would be easy."

I replied, "Yes you can make a great deal of money but don't mistake this for a get-rich-quick-scheme because it definitely is not that. What else do you want?" I asked him what he had done before and he said he'd done counselling for many years and that he loved it. I asked what he loved about it and he said he loved helping people to make improvements in their lives. *Good* I thought, and I pointed out how, when he gets a team to work with, he would enjoy supporting his team in a similar way.

I wanted to explore how he could bring who he is and what he's passionate about, to this business. Because on the surface, one would think one is simply selling products but this isn't the case. It's only the tiniest bit of what we're actually doing.

We explored other things he wanted but all the while I could feel he had not yet decided to do the business. Eventually I said: "You haven't decided": (Level Two).

He said he thought he had. After all, he had paid for his starter pack and was using the products himself every month. In other words because he had made the investment, he thought that meant he had committed.

I said, "No…the reason things are not working out is because you haven't yet decided. And who in their right mind, would follow a person who isn't dyed-in-the-wool to what they're doing? People usually follow someone who is committed and clear about where he is going. Commitment isn't the time you put in but the line you cross. You haven't crossed that line yet."

I shared with him my story of going to Diamond, which is a successful level in my company. (See next chapter). I told him how I'd been hovering around the target for five months and presumably I was *going for Diamond* every month. When asked by my Mentors if this was the month — I would always answer *Yes* but something inside was missing and I was not fully engaged. However, on March 1st, 2007, I woke up knowing I was going Diamond that month. — It arose from within — not from my head as a good idea but from my heart and soul. It had been decided and sure enough I became Diamond that month.

What was the difference between the earlier months and that month? It wasn't that I was closer to the target from the volume point of view. No, I had been there for five months. It was as if the connection to my heart happened, not just the connection to my head. But how do you access that — you may ask.

He said, "You mean I haven't decided."

"Yes…" I said, "you haven't decided."

"Well then, how do I decide?" he asked.

I said, "You don't…it happens by grace when the time is right. You can prepare for it but you cannot will it."

"What do you mean?" He was puzzled.

"You see it's like *my will* and *Thy will* — which one are you working for?" I wanted to know if it was just about him making a lot of money. What would touch, move and inspire others to be part of his purpose? Was it financial freedom for the many? If it was just about him it was not motivating.

Readiness is not under your jurisdiction; it's part of the great mystery…But willingness is under your control…I can show you how to improve your level of willingness. How to set your intention; actions you will need to take and things to think about. The more centred in your heart you are, the sweeter it will be. This will prepare you for and hopefully even quicken the decision. It's almost like we **think** we have made the decision but we have to **know** the higher purpose for the decision to stick. And if you're not sure, look at your results.

You see, I never asked to do Relationship Marketing. In fact, I was adamantly opposed to it. No, really!! The person who brought me into the business had a very big job on her hands because I told her several times I had no interest whatsoever in doing this business. But through her tenacious commitment and perseverance, she was able to put me in front of her team. She knew my vision and she knew what I needed.

After that, I was on board. And if you were to ask me why I am doing this business, I would say because I was on the precipice of change and the decision was made before my head got around to it. How do I know that I am supposed to be doing it? Because I am doing it. And I finally surrendered to the fact that it was happening regardless whether I was kicking and screaming and resistant or not. Think about the times in your life where you didn't want to do something — and you really objected but somehow it happened anyway. And then a whole new world opened up beyond anything you could have imagined sitting on the outside looking in.

"So, in a way you're off the hook," I said.

He got it right away — he knew it was the truth and in a way it was liberating for him.

He let out a big sigh of relief.

After all what use is beating yourself up going to do? Telling yourself there's something wrong. Sure there are actual practical things you can do to be hugely successful in this business and there are some excellent books that will help. Sure you can push your way, buy your way, pressure your way, nearly kill your way to success. But whether it sticks or not, depends on your readiness. The sweet spot comes with true alignment of purpose and mission that connects with others of shared values. Then you may well experience grace and ease.

So yes, you may be able to make it happen but usually this approach is not sustainable.

Now once the DECISION arises — and don't be surprised if it hasn't already happened (even if you don't like the idea), then the job will be how to get over yourself enough to proceed. For this journey will bring up anything in the way of you fulfilling your dreams and offering your gifts and talents to the world.

A point I would like to make here is that even if you cannot imagine being a "Network Marketer" as your dream career, what if you put two to three years in with all your might. You could reap the benefits of a residual income for the rest of your life while you do what you really came to Planet Earth to do. Something to think about.

For instance, one of the leaders on my team has the dream to support artists to live their art in the world. — What do most artists need? Money. So once the financial vehicle is working well, it frees up time to do that which you love. And the people she is attracting share in this purpose and many are artists and musicians.

My dream is my Retreat Centre and working with people to transform their lives and bring their gifts and talents out to the world and get paid for it. I am now living that journey. I am writing books, riding my horse, and because I put the years required to build a great business, I am now reaping the rewards because the business is a vehicle for transformation.

This may seem like a big task and it is but it does happen, one step at a time, with incredible support. This is the nature of this business.

So how's this sounding so far?

How do you find out at what level a person is? And by the way, people at Level 3 can build a fairly impressive business; the distinction is in taking it up to the next level. Help them find their readiness.

Listen, listen, listen, and learn about them. People reveal themselves to us very quickly. Use the famous F.O.R.M. questioning format to find out about them. F=Family, O=Occupation, R=Recreation, and M=Motivation. Find out what dream is still on their hearts, yet to be fulfilled.[7]

Signs of Readiness:

- They have passion in their words and actions.
- They are leaning forward and curious.
- They have a clear vision they are committed to fulfilling
- They're less caught up in tiny details and fears.
- You sense that they have some insight.
- They are connected to the essence, even with limited understanding.
- They are on the precipice of change. They will tell you, so make sure to listen up closely.
- They are sick and tired of being broke or sick of being unhealthy, unfulfilled etc…or sick of a certain situation or way of life.
- They are done with the level they have reached in the business thus far.

7   www.janedeuber.com

- They are no longer whining or complaining but are sincerely looking for empowerment.
- They trust you and will take a look at what you are offering. I often invite people to just come and take a look and after that they will know for sure if it resonates with them or not.
- You can tell their heart; head, emotions, and intentions are engaged.
- Objections are minimal. Even if they don't have the time or money, they will find ways to overcome any perceived problems.
- You know them well enough to be very strong and insistent that they have to take a look, and they do (even if they are kicking and screaming all the way there, like I was).
- Because they have a strong desire, they do not use excuses or blame anyone or anything for their circumstances.

Have you ever bought a book and it sits on the shelf at home for years? Or perhaps you browsed it once but were not ready to understand the content.

Then one day, the book literally begs you to pick it up again. You read its content and suddenly you comprehend the jewels inside. Wow...so even though you had it in your possession — you were not ready to read it.

Things click and flow when a person is ready to change.

I have to say one of my absolute favorite things is working with people who are ready now. Success loves speed and with a person who is ready you can create traction fast in this business. I encourage you to look for people, who are ready in their lives with a vision and knowledge of why they are doing it now. For those of you who have already built a substantial team, dig deep into your organization and find the new people — there you will find this readiness and passion.

Are you ready?

Chapter 23

Template for Success

To illustrate the previous lessons from Chapter 22, I am sharing my personal story of reaching one of the company's highest levels. I had attended a *Go Diamond Leadership* Training in Portland when I discovered the Template for Success that I have used many times since. I hope you can relate it to your situation and glean inspiration from it.

Standing up at the Go Diamond Training in Portland, with about 350 other attendees, I declared:

"I'm going Diamond this month."

The leader who was facilitating the program looked intently at me for clarification and I repeated, "Yes, I'm going Diamond… this month."

He stepped to the edge of the stage, looking directly at me. "It looks like she means it," he commented.

There was a certainty he could see and that I could feel in every cell of my being that had not been present before. Diamond is a very high level of leadership in my business. Over the five previous months, I was well in range to hit the target but for some reason I hadn't quite decided that it was time. When asked by my sponsor, I always said, "Yes I am ready," but what I should have said was, "Yes I am willing." Readiness had not been present even though I was taking all the right action steps.

But on this day as I stood there, a calm energy and knowing prevailed.

Later that same day, I experienced an epiphany that set the stage for this to happen.

I set off from Portland at 12:15 p.m. with the thought: *I want to be on the 6:30 p.m. ferry to Bowen Island.*

Driving home from Portland to Bowen Island, where I live on the West Coast of Canada, would normally take a good six and a half to seven hours, with a busy Sunday border crossing and unknown traffic. To boot, my daughter phoned and asked if I would stop by a feed store on the way home to pick up grain for the horses. Because our usual store would be closed when I crossed the border, she suggested I pull off somewhere in the States.

Seventy miles an hour on a freeway isn't really conducive to looking and sensing farm areas for feed. I did pull off and drive into the country a way when I thought, *What am I doing? I need help from my team.* So I phoned my daughter and put the ball back in her court suggesting she Google it. "Good idea," she responded. I got myself back on the freeway, heading north when she called and gave me specific directions.

It was a wonderful feed store with all kinds of lovely horsey distractions, which almost made me lose sight of my quest. Suddenly I remembered my focus, loaded up the grain, and took off so as not to hinder my plan.

Was it reasonable to think that I could catch that ferry? On one hand yes, it was within range, but then again, no, because it was a little tight and there could be all kinds of conditions that might impair this, including a border crossing …But I was certain of doing it, so I dismissed any thought or suggestion from the mind such as; *I should give up on the idea.*

I drove within the speed limit (well almost) and stayed totally focused. Picking up gas when needed and drinking the products my company provided that supported nourishment and mental clarity, allowed me to keep going. For the most part, the traffic was smooth and I was consumed with the mission of getting on that ferry.

Thoughts and reflections of the weekend passed in and out of my mind and I chuckled in amusement as I remembered I had made a bold statement about going Diamond this month in front of hundreds of people. In my mind, I went over the feeling in my body of that level of certainty and specifically how it felt. It felt real. It felt true.

As I approached the border, the line-up was heavy but I would still not allow the mind to cancel my plan of the 6:30 p.m. ferry. And boy, the ego mind sure tried. I stayed focused, looking ahead — imagining the line-up moving fast. And sure enough it did. The cars were going through the border so effortlessly it amazed me.

I left the border at 5:38 p.m. and wanted to think this was crazy — there was no way I could catch the ferry but I simply would not allow the thought to be constructed in my mind at all.

Driving consciously, deliberately; alert as an owl watching its prey, I felt like I was in a light beam. It was a game I was playing and I was having fun with it.

I arrived on the dot of 6:30 at the ticket booth and suddenly remembered the ten-minute cut off rule. Whoops, I had forgotten about that. The attendant had the right to refuse me, since you really were supposed to be there ten minutes early to board. However, she gave me a quizzical look but without comment handed me the ticket and announced into her headset, "Last car coming through."

I drove down into the terminal and right onto the ferry that was almost loaded. Turning off the key, I closed my eyes and thought, **"That's it, that's my template for Diamond."**

All month I held myself in this level of focus and certainty. There were a few contractions in the last week but I never let myself off the hook for a moment. It was going to happen. And it was going to happen with ease and grace. I didn't have to kill myself or anyone else in the process — it simply wanted to happen.

But I did have to keep my mind in check. If it wandered off and tried to scare me, I simply took myself for a walk and remembered that it was a game. All I had to do was serve others.

On the last week, my numbers were not as high as I would have liked but I wouldn't let any doubt creep in. I simply remembered the feeling of driving the car through to the 6:30 ferry successfully that day — and feeling the certainty of knowing that no other option was possible.

One day though, just before I was to go in and work with a new associate, I felt anxiety creeping in — panic: *Oh my God is this really going to happen?* For a moment I had forgotten it was a game. So I went outside and called my up-team support person. She ever so graciously reminded me of the truth once again and quickly, I came back home into myself. Feeling peace and gratitude, I proceeded on with love, focus, and service. The only way to succeed in this business is truly to serve others. As my focus shifted back onto, *whom can I serve today?* The anxiety fell away.

I mused at the idea of being unattached to the outcome yet certain of the result. How did this fit in with my spiritual quest? I laughed and once again remembered it was a game I was playing and if it didn't happen I wouldn't die — I would be ok...I reconciled this within myself by remembering my original reason for getting on board. I had to remind myself of the greatness of the products; the miracles I had seen over the sixteen months of being involved with this company; The transformation I had seen in the people I was playing this game with…and the love and connectedness I felt every day. I felt the gratitude well up again from deep within and knew I was on track and on purpose.

At 2:00 p.m. on the 31st of March 2007 – as planned, my team arrived at Diamond. Oh what fun and rejoicing followed.

The next day, I was asked; "What was more exciting; to see your team meet their targets or going to Diamond?"

I have to be honest; hitting Diamond was awesome but my heart was the most engaged and my spirit the most lifted to see my team meet their targets. I loved the work, the patience, the lessons, and the heart-felt connections that occurred as this team came together to support one another.

The decision to go Diamond happened first. Then it took action, dedication, incredible team support, magic, and focus.

Deep down I wondered if it was "my" decision at all.

Chapter 24

Expectations and Perceptions

In this business, it is all about perception and expectations, especially with respect to whom you will attract into your Tribe. It's almost uncanny when you see the mirrors that show up on your team. We tend to attract what we expect, so pay close attention to your expectations. The road to success is paved with many challenges. Meeting those challenges has ten percent to do with reality or what happens and ninety percent to do with how we deal with it. It's almost irrelevant what happens but our thinking minds can sabotage our efforts by making a mountain out of a molehill, to screw things up.

There was a man on my team who had a European accent and was convinced that people in this country did not give credit to him because of his accent. When I first met him I was so impressed with his feisty spirit and his credentials. He had credibility with me right away and I would have believed him and been open to his business invitation even though I had just met him. I didn't even register his accent. Unfortunately he was fixated on his story of having an accent and not being respected. He was certain the business would be hard for him to do and guess what — it was.

I always loved this little parable.

There once was a couple of travellers visiting from a far-away country. They were greeted at the castle gateway by the king. Upon their arrival they asked the king, "What are the people like in your country?"

The king turned the questions back to them. "Well what are the people like in your country?"

The travellers responded, "Closed, suspicious, rather self-centred, and small minded."

"Oh," the king replied, "you'll find them to be the same here."

Two weeks later, another couple of travellers entered through the same gateway and saw the king sitting by a tree, looking happy and calm. They inquired, "What are the people like in your country?"

Again the king asked them the same question, "What are the people like in your country?"

The travellers replied with, "Oh they are very kind, open-minded, respectful, and courteous."

The king responded with a big smile on his face, "You will find them to be the same here."

The moral of the story is: Whatever you expect to find, you will find.

I'll never forget this dream my daughter had when she was little. She said, "There was an old disfigured man at the retreat centre. He really was in a bad way with a hunched back and engorged face." She said that she wanted to run from this man because she was afraid of how he looked and then suddenly she saw our dog Billy run over and greet him with as much zest and devotion as he shows everyone else. The man reached down to stroke Billy and Billy, with his tail waggling, gave him a big lick across his face. It brought tears to my daughter's eyes as she thought of how non-judgmental Billy was. Soon, she was able to go over and speak with this man, who despite being disfigured was kind and full-hearted.

In the Tribe you will have such a variety of people. Sometimes I affectionately think of us as the motley crew because this business attracts all kinds of souls. It is important to remember to watch out for your judgments of them. You will be surprised by the ones you think will soar and they don't and the ones you think will do nothing and they soar. At the same time, it is important to not expect sudden and immediate change. For example, if you have Sheep on your team, do not to expect them to become Dogs overnight. They may quickly change, however, unless they are doing some serious personal development work, they probably will not.

What's more, they don't need to change, although change is the possibility. The Tribe core-resonating values are about the variety and seeing and accepting people for who they are. Instead look at the wonderful qualities Sheep have and go with that. Sheep are courteous and wonderful creatures.

Just because we see potential in people, doesn't mean it will be realized. Relax, breathe, and watch for the very best in people. Whatever we focus love and blessings upon expands. Ultimately, we will be peaceful and more effective when we allow our Tribe members to be who they are.

Chapter 25

Volunteer Leadership

Some say leaders are born but I would say; *Leaders are carved by the challenges they live through and their free flowing instincts.* Volunteer Leadership is about people waking up with a passion for contribution and a heart dedicated to service.

In Relationship Marketing, you do not hire or fire anyone. Therefore it is purely an art to understand and appreciate how to inspire and create results with your Tribe. A big part of that is to invite out to play the gifts and talents that may be hidden dormant in a person. As you study the previous chapters, you will glean the insights of how to work with your Tribe.

In Relationship Marketing, money flows beyond hour for dollar as you create duplication with your team. Duplication happens with a system, a method of operation and each company uses a slightly different one. You get paid residual income indirectly through building a network that pays bonuses and commissions on a monthly basis. A new associate in my business said to me one day, "I feel bad and want to pay you for your help. You've assisted me so much." I knew in that moment that I hadn't explained to her very well how this business works. Coming from the corporate model, she didn't realize that Relationship Marketing was the antithesis of what she was used to. I let her know she didn't have to pay me and that I was getting paid. I showed her the compensation plan and how I was rewarded by helping her. In fact, it is the only way we get paid; by helping others to do what they want. It is a brilliant and fair model and I love it.

Where else can we move with our gifts and talents so deliberately? And how does it affect the whole? This model of doing business encourages us to step up to the plate and take leadership — even when sometimes leadership means being a really great follower or support person. To illustrate how this works, here is an example:

At a nine-day leadership training I attended many years ago with my best friend Chrystalle, there were in attendance seventy outstanding entrepreneur women, from around the world. I was so intimidated at first; it took me three days to show up with my whole self. By the nature of the process, I got C-sectioned in and boy did I learn some tough lessons.

On one of the final days, we were given a big assignment but we had a small window of time to accomplish it. We were driven to a nearby school, in a poor district, which needed a serious physical makeover. Tasks included were: Clearing stones and rocks from an entire playing field; fixing the deep potholes in the large parking areas; installing an underground irrigation system across an indoor and outdoor garden area; building large, wooden plant containers and planting them with seeds, flowers, and herbs. We also had to put a zigzagged pavement in across the playground and build a small wall around the office area.

Arriving early in the morning, we could see from the bus all the materials and equipment waiting for us. There were even large tractors and backhoes for our use. It was a daunting proposition and a boiling- hot, August day.

Although we wondered if it was possible to accomplish, we barely had time to think about it. Instead, we witnessed the miracle of a group with a mission. As the team mobilized, it was like poetry in motion. The first part was to establish who had what skill base and what were our individual strengths. As the various small groups were being put together, we needed a person who understood carpentry as well as how to install an irrigation system.

Chrystalle had these skills in spades and knew what to do but was reluctant to step forward and take the lead. She always preferred the support role. I knew she knew what to do and looked over to her to see if she would take up the baton and lead us. She caught my glance and knew what I was thinking. As the inquiry of who had this skill was ramping up, she finally stepped forward.

It was eloquent to watch as Chrystalle led seventy women to various tasks throughout the day. I loved watching her shining in her strength, as I became one of her followers. It was a reverse from our usual roles at my retreat centre and this experience changed me so profoundly that day. It foreshadowed a different reality that would be needed in our new business venture.

In many cases, the usual leader types had to toe the line and become followers, doing whatever was asked of them. Some had trouble coming down off their high horses of importance or getting their manicured hands dirty (Peacocks). But they did and it was beautiful to behold.

The impossible happened that day at that school and even the kids could not believe we were doing this for them, for free. After school, they came running out and joined in to help us. It was a day I will always remember. We may have been exhausted but we all felt elated because we had worked together, worked hard, and got everything accomplished. It made a really big difference in these kids' lives and it changed us forever.

This is exactly how Relationship Marketing works; the same method of working together for a common vision. There is no boss and you cannot hire or fire anyone. It's therefore a remarkable volunteer team. You get to step up and take leadership

because you decide to and because it's the smart thing to do —
not because it's in your job description.

Together We Have it All

No matter what the members of your Tribe say, they will always
be changing their minds. They'll have big dreams and plans but
will fall short of the mark. I'm not saying this as a downer or to
be cynical but as a way of bringing awareness to the situation.
It's not that this is bad; it's just that there are so many moving
parts for everything to align into perfect order. Most people don't
have the capacity to contain their dreams and this is where, if
done right, this profession can play a major role. Since the Tribe is
made up of many different types of people with a variety of skill
bases, we can work together and all look good. For instance when
I first started, I was terrible at filling in forms and other system-
related activities. My daughter said I had *formaphobia* and I should
get over it. Well it took me quite a while but if my success had
depended on that — I would have been screwed. Instead, my
wonderful sponsor had those skills in spades and filled them in
for me for quite a while. In the meantime, she set me loose to
meet and connect with people, which was my strength. Then one
day, just as she was about to kick me out of the nest, I felt ready
to fill in the forms. When I did, I had to laugh at how ridiculously
easy it was.

Another Quick Example

I was listening to an on-line training the other day and there was
the typical technology glitch. It took about fifteen minutes before
the system was up and running properly. In the meantime, there
were about fifty people on a phone line waiting. I thought to
myself, *I wonder who will step up as a leader and use the time to connect*

with the people on the phone. I waited and waited and waited. I was just about to step in, when someone on my team spoke up and created a small activity. It was enjoyable and kept people involved enough to wait out the time. I was pleased to see how she had blossomed as a leader recently. You see, nobody makes you a leader. You have to step up and claim it. Life is constantly inviting us to lead but many do not see themselves as the one. All you have to do is say, *Yes. Why not me?*

The power and everything you need is in the Tribe. Holding space long enough to allow a more reluctant person to contribute is an aptitude we could all adopt. It's like the mother who always thinks it's easier for her to do the job than to let the six-year-old do it. Let them do it. Allow them to make a mess and learn. It's important for you to contribute to the team yourself because you play an integral part. To say one member is more valuable than another is inaccurate and short-sighted. You will find everything you need in the whole Tribe — not one person left out.

Once, I was asked how much time I put into my business. I responded, "Twenty-four hours a day, seven days a week." At first, they thought I must be a workaholic but I explained to them that I have integrated it into my life so much that it is part of me. If you're married, are you married part-time or for a certain number of hours a week? No it's all the time. That's how I feel about my business. As you develop your business and get to know your Tribe, you start to care for people and this is forever.

I have never found a more perfect vehicle to transport us into this new realm. Relationship Marketing has it all. It is relevant to today's changing economy. And we are waking up whether we are ready to or not. If you stay the course and move in the direction of successful actions, you will naturally be guided along the way.

Sharing your talents and gifts in service to others opens the flow of unlimited abundance. The more people you serve, the greater the experience and results. As you really get the essence of people and love them, they blossom. Lead the way by showing them how to hold themselves accountable to their highest and best. I can assure you, you will be fulfilled beyond your wildest dreams.

Are you ready to bring forth your talents and gifts and volunteer them to the Tribe and to the world?

Chapter 26

More Great Reasons to Take this Path of Relationship Marketing

There are so many great reasons to have a Relationship Marketing business. There are the obvious reasons of creating a great livelihood, time freedom, and tax benefits. Then there are more hidden reasons and once you achieve mastery of them you are free to really create the world you want. I have asked people — if they could get over the fear of what people think of them, would this be worthwhile? Many say yes; this alone would be worth it. What if you could learn to speak in public, without fear or embarrassment? What if you could earn a residual income doing what you love?

When I first started my business, it didn't take long before I realized this wasn't about product sales. It was about something far greater and to me, this was a challenge that was compelling. Yet it could not happen effectively without brilliant products. So right off the bat, let's assume you have found the company worthy of your dedication and loyalty.

One day, I was thinking about my daughter who was, at the time, a student at UBC and working really, really hard. I asked her once how she felt about being a student and she said, "I love it because it is taking me where I want to go." In her case, this was to be a veterinarian and it was at that point, I had an, *ah ha* moment.

I started thinking about the mind-set of Relationship Marketing. How we stand in it and how people view it. I thought the mistake many people make is that they think they are going to 'sell products' for the rest of their lives. Thus, when they present it to others, they are asking them to join them in the same feat. In most cases this does not exactly fit in with how they pictured their lives. Of course they wouldn't want to do it any more than my daughter wouldn't want to be a student forever.

Malcolm Gladwell's book *Outliers* says "In fact, researchers have settled on what they believe is the magic number for true expertise: ten thousand hours." That is between five to seven years. The beauty of Relationship Marketing is you can study your profession while earning a great deal of money.

Imagine loving the profession because it is taking you where you want to go. What if you thought of it as your university degree and devoted three to five years to achieve it? At the end of it you will have received great business experience; an unparalleled personal development program that you could not pay enough money to receive; a residual income that is willable; you'll have improved the lives of thousands and created a wonderful community of friends. Oh, and did I mention, time and money freedom that will allow you to do that which you came to Planet Earth to do? Does that reframe it or what? You see it is simply the vehicle for your ultimate dream, not the dream itself. Now there are exceptions to any rule and there are those few people who totally dig it and want to do it forever just as there are people who stay students forever.

The idea of residual income is that you can eventually retire, with a caveat that Continuing Education is required, as in any degree program. In Relationship Marketing, that means keeping your thoughts and energy clean and clear and overseeing your business as a Mentor because you would have duplicated yourself many times over.

But who is willing to do a PhD or even get a diploma in this profession? Any smart person, I would say. I am finding more and more young people jumping on board to get the money thing handled so they can be free to do what they love to do.

There are some really important factors that can make or break your success. Here are a few:

1. It is no mistake that you have been drawn into this business.

What if I told you that absolutely everything that is going on in your business is perfect and exactly as it is suppose to be, and that there is no problem?

That's right you are not a failure. You are exactly where you're supposed to be. Some of you will read this and let out a big sigh of relief. Others of you may get your hackles up and say, *what the heck is she talking about?* But realize the viewpoint I bring is through the window of personal and professional development.

There is an overtone that plays along with us in our lives. We have our up-front life, our roles, the place we live, and we do what we do. This is what we think is our life. Yet there is a whole other undercurrent that is operating in our lives simultaneously... And it brings to us all that we need, to evolve by way of teachings, tests, and challenges.

These challenges don't come to punish us, or to tell us we're idiots — they come as an invitation; an opportunity to expand, to grow, and to open. And if we can look at our business in terms of the gift that is being brought into our lives right now by these challenges, then we will be in alignment with a higher plan for us.

If you look at your business right now — Are you happy with the results? Maybe not but take a closer look and see the path along the way that brought you to where you are. Notice the clues and messages unfolding in front of you and see if you can identify a deeper meaning. Sit back, reflect, and take a moment to discover what these clues are. What has life been trying to show you through this process of Relationship Marketing? Where do you need to be more open and coachable? You will find many answers as you go back and study Part One of this book.

2. Handling Disappointments

I think one of the most difficult things about this profession, as in life, is navigating disappointment. And this is where most people get taken out. It usually happens around a situation where a plan is made and then the phone call comes in and the plans get cancelled. If we are not accepting and even expecting change on a regular basis — we are heading for a lot of grief.

There are a lot of theories out there that we create our own reality by our thinking and belief systems. I personally see that when we change our thinking, we change our world and this isn't always easy. Hence this is the self-actualization component of this business.

Just the other day, I got a phone call from a friend saying she had changed her mind about a business trip we had booked together. The airline tickets had been purchased and hotels were booked, etc. I had been really looking forward to hanging out having fun with her, in between the speakers at the conference. The part that upset me the most was I actually got the news first via an email from someone else before my friend phoned me. I was taken by surprise and felt a heavy ache of disappointment.

Instead of making anyone wrong, I let myself feel the disappointment deeply. I took the time to realize that it wasn't just about this particular situation but really was about the depth and breadth of disappointment that was already within me. Not to minimize that particular situation but somehow it felt like a deeper healing from the past was happening. Either way, it was what it was. Suffering comes from not accepting reality as it is. I don't have to like it but here it is. The important thing here is to feel the disappointment as it is arising. Take the time with it. I've known times in my life where disappointment has taken me out for weeks, months, and even years. This is because I didn't give it my full attention so it sat in the background as this lingering pain.

How many times do we invite a person to a presentation and they promise to come but then cancel at the last minute? What about bringing a person into the business and they have all these great dreams but give up on themselves so quickly? How many times have you been happy to find a fantastic potential business partner — but they cannot see the bigger picture and leave before getting started?

I have seen many people get discouraged and walk away just when they were about to break through and I have seen people quit at the first sign of rain. Disappointment is rampant and it shows up with fellow teammates, partners — and especially in ourselves. Since it is part of life and part of this business, we need to learn how to make lemonade when given lemons.

So what do I do now when it happens?

STEP ONE

As I said, it's important to feel and acknowledge disappointment when it arises. Literally sit with it and give it your full attention. Like all feelings when they are given life by our awareness, they are satisfied and don't create havoc in our lives. If we stuff them down, or deny this feeling and jump to Step Two before completing Step One, disappointment will probably surface again and often inappropriately.

Disappointment is one of the biggest killers of people's dreams and talents. If we do not give attention to this feeling when it arises, it internalizes and often will build up a case as to why this is not the right business for us. Who wants to sit in disappointment? Nobody, but the fact is, if it is there, it needs your attention. Nobody else's attention will do. You will usually find when you go deeper that it leads to another disappointment that happened earlier on in your life. You may even discover a theme that has been playing out throughout your life. If this happens, then, great — you are on to something important. Oh by the way, did I mention this was a self-actualization program?

Too many disappointments that are not met with understanding can very quickly sabotage our businesses and may lead to depression.

STEP TWO

Coming back to peace requires getting present again in your body. A quick way to do this is to sit in nature. Nature is totally present and will help you, if you tune in to the stillness and space of it. This is my favourite thing to do. I always feel so peaceful and happy when I do this, even for ten or twenty minutes.

I will go and clean a barn or hike with my dog to the lake. I'll breathe some fresh air and become present to the environment. Suddenly I am wondering — What problem?

You can also phone your up-team person to assist you through it. Remember, when you are down go up to the up-team leaders and when you are up, go down and share your happy spirit.

Another approach is *The Work of Byron Katie*,[8] in which she shows you, through inquiry — four simple questions. It teaches how to question the story the mind is telling you, then turn it around into

---

8   The Work of Byron Katie. www.thework.com

freedom. I highly recommend going on line and following her instructions in *The Work*.

STEP THREE

Often, some clarity will start to surface at this point and we see the perfection of the situation. In the case of the friend who cancelled on me, I knew my friend couldn't afford it and that actually, she was making the right decision to cancel. She apologized to me for how I had received the news. Her intention had been to call me before the other person sent the email. It was a genuine timing error, so I could relax and trust that my friend did not intend to cause any suffering.

What else can you do?

After I have sat with the disappointment and let it be ok, I sometimes contact the person and talk it through.

Make other phone calls — only after you have completed Step One. You'll know if you have completed it by the level of peacefulness in your mind and body.

Make lemonade out of lemons.

This now leads to another major lesson that can make or break your success:

3. Non-attachment to the Outcome

Wow, I've never seen a better spiritual practice than learning non-attachment with the people you work with…especially in Relationship Marketing.

I realized one day as I was trying to make my Deer be an Eagle that I was pushing her beyond where she wanted to go, (in that moment anyway). This had created conflict between us for years and because we cared about each other, this behaviour caused a lot of angst. It's quite the delicate matter when you think your job is to manage your Tribe. I was either being pushy or I withdrew my energy all together. As you can imagine, in both cases I was creating separation. It didn't feel good and it was totally ineffective.

Today, I have learned I am not a manager but an equal member of the Tribe. I now work more to be peaceful and effective. How I do this is to be realistic with people; to be here for them, if and when, they are ready. I continue to love them and keep an open heart and mind, no matter what. I'm not perfect and I forget now and again, especially when I see potential so blatantly right in front of my face. The only problem is — it's for them to see and use, no matter what I want. The timing has to line up and they have to be ready. Remember it's about the growth and expansion being offered in each moment. It's about unleashing the potential, which is an art. It's a dance between seeing, inspiring, and trusting the unfolding. And running like heck with the ones who are ready to go now!

Well, for that alone, this is a brilliant business. Imagine having all the opportunity in the world to be non-attached to the outcome, every single day; playing with who shows up; loving people just right where they are. It's actually easy. The caveat for me now is they have to want success more than I want it for them. In other words. they have to meet me halfway. And that is freedom for us both.

4. Resilience

Resilience is a *must have* if you are to succeed in this business. You see, the game changes along the way and you have to pay attention to what is coming or, in some cases, to what just happened. Corporate changes, products change, markets change, the economy changes, and people change. And you have to have a certain level of willingness to do something about it if you can, or to go with it if you cannot. And of course I'm not talking about deal-breakers but just the fact that it is the nature of this business for things to change. So just when you thought you had it all figured out and things were going tickety boo, be prepared. Things will change. Get used to it. In fact, welcome it.

Adaptability and resilience are today's requirements to have a sane and happy life. Trust that there is a divine plan unfolding and tune into it, rather than fighting or resisting it. Don't give up on yourself or your Tribe or your company. Go the distance, pay attention, and surrender to the waves of change.

Chapter 27

It Really Is Important to Do Your Thing

The person who brought me into the business was told repeatedly that she was crazy bringing someone in who lived in Canada on a small island with 4000 people. They coached her to find people in larger areas with populations of at least a million. "Find someone who lives in the city where it, apparently, is all happening," they said.

She responded: *"No, I know* Angelyn and I know her vision and I know her dream and I know her thing. She is a leader and I'm betting my time and money on her." (Thank you for believing in me, Renee.)

When I first started the business I thought I really should get an apartment in Vancouver so that I could be a leader in the city. After all, who can build a significantly large business on an island? And so I did. I rented a beautiful, elegant, attic apartment atop a grand mansion, in a rich location. I showed up for work on Monday morning and left on Friday afternoon. For the first week or two, the novelty was fun and I tripped around all the local cafes and bookstores in the evening.

One day, I woke up with a pain in my heart and felt unhappy. I couldn't quite figure out what was happening because my business was going great and I was doing what I thought I 'should' do.

The source of my pain was that I longed to be home in nature with my animals. It wasn't my thing to be in the city. I started to think of how duplicable this was for others living in more remote areas. Could they afford apartments in the city? I wanted to think this could be for everyone, especially since now we have such great technology. Then it dawned on me that actually it is a home-based business and... what was I thinking? I had left the very place I was privileged to enjoy with this kind of business.

The following month I gave my notice and never looked back.

So what is your thing?

Not just where you want to live but what you love to do. Are you doing your thing?

Many people tell me they do not know what their gifts and talents are and because I speak so much about this, they feel a little left behind or out of the loop.

The best way I can describe it is: What is your THING? What are you passionate about? What makes you forget what day or hour it is because you are so inspired and focused? When are you the happiest?

When are you lost almost in another dimension? Don't judge what it may be, just get in touch with it.

In context of the animal characteristics and phases, what are the Dog and Dolphin's thing? They love playing and being great cheerleaders for your dream and vision. Good, then this is the perfect business for them.

Eagles, Dolphins, Beavers and Lynx are usually great at the front of the room. It's their thing to communicate their message really well. Whereas Cat, Deer, Mouse, and Sheep prefer to be in the background, making sure the room is set up and running smoothly with all the details. They relish this support role. It is their thing. Again, this is another reflection of how effective the whole Tribe is together. When we do our own unique things and trust that it all gets taken care of — it does. It's perfection.

Our thing is the true sweet spot that we feel when we do what we love. It hardly takes any effort because it truly is a gift.

I do encourage people to find a place in nature to sit in silence and get to know their deepest dreams and gifts. Even if you are in the city, life will still speak to you there. Have you ever noticed how you may be trying to figure something out and suddenly you find your answer on a billboard as you go by on a bus? It's as if life stops and points you to something and you suddenly become aware of the message. Even cloud formations and crazy things that happen right in front of you, are often symbols or messages.

The more present we are in life, the more we will feel this wonderful, gentle and sometimes not so gentle, guidance. Once you find your thing it's important to commit to it.

Commitment isn't the time you put in, it's the line you cross — I saw this slogan once on one of the Whistler/Blackcomb Billboard signs and immediately I adopted it. It's so true. In rock climbing, commitment means: *choose and move.* You want your instincts tuned in, not the mind, which wants to analyze the situation and usually ends up talking you out of it. In skiing, when heading off a black diamond run (most difficult), it means leaning down into the mountain. You cannot attempt that level of steepness without surrendering forward — even though it seems counter-intuitive and crazy at first. If you start resisting and leaning back — all kinds of not so good things happen and believe me, it's not pretty.

When you surrender into the mountain, leaning out forward over the skis, you're going to have a more elegant, invigorating, smoother ride. But it takes courage to cross that line. To lean in and let go, to do your thing. Imagine being that committed in your business?

I can usually tell if someone in my team is ALL IN or if they have their little toe in. If they're treating it like a hobby or *we'll wait and see what happens.* It always amazes me when some people actually wonder why they're not successful! When all the time, they have the brake on as they're struggling up a hill. Trust what that deep inner joy wants to express through you.

I sometimes think our path is all figured out already and all we have to do is:

- *Show up and choose to be present.*
- *Pay attention to what has heart and meaning.*
- *Tell the truth without blame or judgment.*
- *Be open to outcome, not attached to outcome*[9]

As you read this now, take a moment to tune into the spaces between the words on these pages. Feel your body on the chair. Take a deep breath, and for a moment or two watch your breath rising and falling. Listen to the sounds in the room or the place you are in right now. And listen to the sounds around you without being consumed by them. Can you feel the stillness deep within and around you? If it is too busy, I suggest letting yourself experience the stillness within the chaos of outside activities. What do you notice? It's in this mindfulness of this present moment that your life opens and transforms. This is what people are looking for; to connect deeply to life and make meaningful connections, to express their truth and live their dreams.

So what is your thing? I encourage you to do your thing — not anybody else's thing.

Putting this business book out with animals and my ideas seemed scary. Yet I know it is courageous to follow my instinct and creativity and to write and share this information. At times, a part of me felt vulnerable. It felt like laying my heart at the altar and opening myself to criticism and ridicule. Believe me, I wanted to sugar coat things to make them more acceptable but I ended up

---

9   Arrien, Angeles. *The Four-Fold Way*. HarperOne, 1993 – www.angelesarrien.com

doing my thing. Someone else would have done it totally differently. Good, It's not their thing. It's my thing to understand what makes people tick and to be close to nature. It's no surprise that the muse found me. I was a willing vessel to carry these ideas out.

So I delivered my thing to you. I am hoping it will trigger or nudge a little part of you out to play. Do your thing. Don't get caught up in other people's rules and ideas. There are so many opinions and rules out there but who cares, if you are following what's true for you. Once and for all, do your thing and manifest it into reality. And why not get paid for doing it?

Your Tribe is waiting for you . . .

PART THREE –
The Potential
of Relationship
Marketing Today

Chapter 28

Old School Thought vs. New School Thought about Relationship Marketing

OLD WAY: It's hard work.

NEW WAY: It takes effort for sure but it becomes easier when you align your business with your vision and purpose. Plus, the effort you put in now, to build your network, pays off in the long term. You're creating an asset for the future.

OLD WAY: Results depend on sales volume at the end of the month.

NEW WAY: Results depend on how relationships and foundations are being developed. How much connection is being made? Points and dollars do not always measure results. How happy are you? How fulfilled are you?

OLD WAY: Customers are stupid and need us to bash them across the head with our sales pitch.

NEW WAY: Customers are intelligent and aware. You simply lay it out and let them choose.

OLD WAY: The products don't matter. It's not about the products or services.

NEW WAY: The quality of products you represent is paramount to creating a solid foundation. It is the integrity of the business.

OLD WAY: It's a business where you lose all your friends.

NEW WAY: If you're not selling or pushing anything on anyone, your friendships should remain intact. Work with the people you love and respect. Best friends who really get what you're doing are great. Maybe you have to build it and they will come. Sometimes they never do and this is perfect. Let go.

OLD WAY: I'll recruit whomever I can get. Hat in hand approach.

NEW WAY: I will carefully select the people I respect and want to work with. When you know what you have in your hands, your level of confidence goes up and your power of influence goes up with it.

OLD WAY: Coming from fear and lack.

NEW WAY: Coming from love and service.

OLD WAY: Go faster and push, needing more volume.

NEW WAY: Whom can I serve today?

OLD WAY: It's a dog eat dog world. Competitive.

NEW WAY: It's a conscious co-operative and win/win system when aligned with a great company worthy of your efforts.

OLD WAY: I have to manage my team to go faster and push them to get results for me.

NEW WAY: You can inspire, support, coach, and educate your team on the systems and ways of this business. You are not their boss or manager.

OLD WAY: You have to be a slick salesperson with a spiel.

NEW WAY: You have to listen, listen, listen. Be authentic, which means being who you are. People buy you first and foremost. You are the gateway. Be transparent.

OLD WAY: It's a pyramid where the rich get richer and the poor get poorer.

NEW WAY: You can advance beyond the person who brought you in; therefore it is not a pyramid. You are the CEO of your own independent business. This is unlike the corporate model where there is only one CEO. You are exchanging products and services; therefore it is not a pyramid. Those who want to get rich, can. Those who want to get their products paid for, can. It's an opportunity where everyone has as much to gain.

OLD WAY: It takes a lot of time.

NEW WAY: Yes it absolutely can and will. The beauty is you can build it fast or slowly. Obviously, the more time you put in, the sooner you will reap the rewards. It can also wrap around your life and you can do it part-time or full-time — just not sometimes. It's designed to give you more time freedom once you've established your network. You get to leverage the time and experience of others. Imagine, as you build your business, having dozens, hundreds and eventually thousands of people working in it. Time and money really get stretched. It will become redolent with ease and grace; where less energy equals more results. (See Lynx).

OLD WAY: It cost a fortune to start your own business.

NEW WAY: That's the beauty of Relationship Marketing. There is a low cost of entry, with vast possibilities and rapid return on your investment.

OLD WAY: It's about the numbers. How many can you recruit? (Ten a day?)

NEW WAY: It's intuitive — go out into the world or on line and attract the people who are looking for you. It's all about resonance and about being of service. Visioning and attraction marketing is today's way.

OLD WAY: Only the lucky few make it to the top.

NEW WAY:	Everyone has as much to gain. The ones who make it to the top are committed and persistent. They are coachable with a spirit of service. They just never give up even when the going gets tough.
OLD WAY:	It's a scam.
NEW WAY:	It's a legitimate and brilliant business model — endorsed by many great influential icons such as: Robert Kiyosaki, Warren Buffett, Donald Trump, and Deepak Chopra, plus many other New Thought leaders.
OLD WAY:	You can throw anything in a bottle and sell one of these systems.
NEW WAY:	If you do that, it won't last. Plus in many cases you need Health Canada and FDA approval.
OLD WAY:	It's a get rich quick scheme.
NEW WAY:	It's the fairest marketing business distribution out there where you have the potential to be rich beyond your wildest dreams. It usually isn't quick though. Sustainability takes endurance and commitment; three to five years to establish your network.
OLD WAY:	It's a job.

NEW WAY: It's your own business and you are your own boss. You have the freedom to design your life the way you want it. Be at home with your kids more. Work only mornings. Choose your own dream team. Get a raise or a holiday whenever you decide.

OLD WAY: If it doesn't work in the first three months, give up.

NEW WAY: Once you've found the right company, you do it until you succeed. (This usually means a minimum of three to five years.)

OLD WAY: Don't be vulnerable.

NEW WAY: Be vulnerable, be authentic, and come from the heart.

OLD WAY: It's about me.

NEW WAY: It's about them.

OLD WAY: It may hurt my ego.

NEW WAY: Yes it absolutely will and that is its job!

Chapter 29

Important Things to Know About this Profession of Relationship Marketing

I was really successful in other businesses I did, but this business I am having difficulty with it...

I cannot do it the old way in this business...it seems to demand a higher level of honesty and transparency...

Unlike other businesses, this business calls me to something way deeper and more authentic...

I cannot hide here.

This business has an instant feedback system...it seems to reflect everything going on inside me. I have to be diligent.

This profession, like no other, offers us a way to grow and serve and be successful, all at the same time. It's as if this business operates under different guidelines or rules and that is what this book will shed some light on.

People think this industry is full of scoundrels, thieves, and liars. And what I would add is; it is full of "hopeful" people who think this is the way that will fix it for them. It is true of any business that you have opportunists and people who really don't care. Sometimes some of these people are incredibly successful in this industry but as with any other form of business, it is not sustainable in the long run.

So having said that, the reason this industry seems to attract a larger number of unique individuals is because it is the highest form of commerce. It's free enterprise to the max. There is a low cost of entry and people still think it is a get rich quick scheme.

My job and commitment is to bring up the standard of this profession and to re-educate people about the evolution that is taking place as the controversy over its business model subsides. We need to understand that the tool is never the culprit; it is the user of the tool who is. How can we use this tool with integrity? What are the principles to consider?

- First thing first: It is imperative to tie your wagon to a winning company that has a proven record, integrity, and a brilliant, consumable product with science and research that is real. Make sure it is a member of the Direct Selling Association and meets the Federal Trade Commission (FTC), Health Canada or your particular country's regulations.

- The Owner/Founder of the Company is important. Their mission and vision emanates through the entire organization. As your Founder goes, so goes the company.

- Like any business, it is a business where 20% of the people do 80% of the work and consequently these are the ones who reap the highest return on their efforts and investment.

- It is also a great system for people wanting to get their products paid for or to earn a couple of hundred extra dollars per month.

- And at the same time, it has an opportunity for vast financial success.

- You do not have to be an expert in any area of this business, if you work with your team. You just have to be coachable, ready, and have your head and heart connected.

- A good system should work for people with the least amount of experience and still be successful, if they follow a simple system and work with the team.

Where things get negative and where the bad reputation comes from, is the disappointment people have, who either do not have the skill, commitment, or wherewithal to do it and to do it right. The barrier to entry is low and people self-select. Many people say they want to own a business but not all follow a success path.

Because it is a process where you are trained by your up team leaders, the duplication system often goes off the rails and causes disappointment and bad results.

It is a simple system that gently massages or sometimes catapults you into the depth of despair only to find out that by going the distance, you have, in fact, developed your ability to know yourself more. Why would anyone intentionally step in to such a void? Because, like the moth to the flame, they cannot help themselves; they are being moved. They are being lured or coerced into expansion. To live with the mundane, tick tock reality of mainstream business, they may never know their potential, much less live it.

I want to be candid because in order to declare yourself into this game, you need to be careful, because it is not for the faint of heart, if you choose to go the whole way. By that, I mean to the highest levels the company has available for you. Or in simple terms, $10,000+ per month. And the further in you choose to go, the more the game amps up. Be true to yourself in an empowered way. Design it with others. Be consistent and give it your highest and best effort.

If you accept the challenge, there are multiple opportunities for growth:

- Learning about patience, perseverance, and tolerance.
- Learning balance.
- Being of service (very rewarding).
- Learning commitment.
- Learning to be a leader.
- To be a better leader.
- To be a great leader.
- Self-actualization.
- Getting over yourself, that is, your own limiting beliefs.
- Expanding your business abilities and skills.
- Being a member of a Network.
- Being with your Tribe.
- Resilience.
- Discernment.
- Public speaking.
- Communications skills.
- Technology — high touch/high tech[10].

Duplication happens with a system, a method of operation and each company uses a slightly different one.

For these things alone, it would be worth it.

---

10   High touch is defined as connecting directly and personally with people, rather than on-line.

Chapter 30

The Potential of Socially Responsible Businesses

What if Robert Kiyosaki is right and Network Marketing is the business of the Twenty-first Century?[11] It's apt that instead of Multi-level Marketing the name now used is Network Marketing or, as I have been referring to it, Relationship Marketing. The use of the word Relationship is the first clue to the changes that are now leading the way in the profession. Relationship Marketing is both high-tech and high touch, a winning combination for home-based business owners. It is about communicating and influencing with integrity, while fostering loyalty and long-term connections. It is blossoming into something distinctly different from its origins.

Today, people want honesty, authenticity, and respect, instead of clichés, hyped-up promises, scripted verbiage, and get-rich-quick-schemes. That way is considered old school and it is what has given this profession a poor reputation in the past. As a result, it has taken decades to uncover its true potential.

This new paradigm is not only a noble way; it simply is the way it works today. The old way of pushing, greed, and manipulation is redundant. The old buttons that you could press for a specific result before, have been disengaged. Even if it appears to work for a while, it will atrophy at lightning speed. Something else is emerging in its place; sustainability, which is the ability of

11   Kiyosaki, Robert. *The Business of the 21st Century.* Manjul Publishing House Pvt. Ltd. 2012

something to last long-term. This comes from a deliberate and conscious connection to what you are doing and with whom you are doing it and of course, with great products and services.

There are so many dimensions to become aware of when you agree to enter this way of commerce. Some are the practical, everyday calendar and activities that move this business forward. Next, there is the building of relationships with a network of like-minded entrepreneurs and interested customers. Then, underneath all the obvious levels, lies the real purpose for each individual. This is the part that has kept me engaged for eight years and gets me out of bed early every single morning. It is the awakening of human consciousness; an evolution that cannot be stopped. It can be avoided but it is happening and the only thing to do is learn the invisible rules of the game. The time has come to wake up once and for all. Relationship Marketing shines a light in the dark and offers a lifeline to freedom.

This evolution causes some people to want to be part of a movement and to connect with their Tribes. This way of working together is never more apparent as when dealing with an upheaval or natural disaster, where everyone rallies together and shares their wealth and skills willingly; where the level of caring gets amped up and people join hands and pool their resources.

What if people could align efforts naturally without a disaster being the catalyst? Imagine opting in to this way of working. Not getting catapulted in by a tragedy but because it is a healthy choice. Today, people are looking for purpose and community and Relationship Marketing provides this, plus right-livelihood, done ethically.

On a service trip to the Dominican Republic I had a direct experience of a functioning tribe. What I noticed reinforced my understanding of the power of community and working together in service. I noticed how even though poverty prevailed conflict was rare between village members. Instead, they looked out for each other.

My western mind thought there should be something wrong with this picture but in fact there was something very much right. There was so much love, peace and acceptance present and I couldn't help but see the stark contrast between my culture and theirs. We have become a culture separated by gated communities, computers, texting, workaholism and TV. I can see the writing on the wall if we do not take stock and look out for each other the way tribes do.

We are at our healthiest as a people in community, not out there as the Lone Wolf. Your contribution is cultivated within the group dynamic. Being witnessed and supported brings about exponential rewards to the whole Tribe.

How you show up in the Tribe, is what attracts people to you. What you believe and how you think puts out a certain energy that people read like a book. *Stay away or let's play.* They notice your transparency, generosity, and genuine desire to serve. What you do and how you do it touches people in a visceral way. At this altitude you cannot hide.

The diversity of your Tribe bodes well in today's changing system of entrepreneurship. When each member plays in his or her strength, something magical happens and the job gets done. Harmony and creativity are rampant in the space of co-operation vs. competition.

When leaders start showing up at every level, something exquisite starts occurring. Greater feats and visions are created. This cooperation and co-creativity builds traction and together, we succeed. There is no other profession where this is so evident as Relationship Marketing. There is a built-in respect factor and you succeed to the degree that you help others succeed. This is the new way; the conscious way of doing business. If I try to manage you, you cannot grow and I will burn out. If I do it for you, you cannot learn. If we work in our strengths together in an environment of contribution — the Tribe thrives.

If this excites and inspires you, I encourage you to knuckle down with your Company and take the time to develop your skills and support your Tribe.

Chapter 31

Being in Love with this Business

Many years ago, I had a brush with Network Marketing and vowed never to go near it, ever again. I believed all the old-paradigm thinking about what it was and was absolutely shocked to find myself saying, "Ok I'll give it a year and see what happens."

I already knew the products were brilliant and wanted to order them but to actually take part in the business was a stunning change of mind and heart. Ten years later, I have found myself deeply fulfilled and successful beyond my wildest dreams.

What I have found is that it is so much more than what I thought I signed up for. It truly is a self-actualizing workshop with a compensation plan and quite frankly, that is the part of the business closest to my heart. I'm not saying all companies out there are good and ethical — you will have to sort the wheat from the chaff and find the right one for you. I'm not saying it is easy but I will say it is worthwhile. My personal experience is with a company and team that have shown a loyalty of purpose, a steadfast commitment, and a passion for this business that ranks us one of the most integrous companies out there.

Being in love with this business, not in resistance but in love, is the name of the game.

You may ask: So how can I be in love with this business if I am not? How does a counterfeit of love work?

The mind doesn't know the difference between real or imagined but certainly the heart does and it is the heart that knows the way. Let your heart pick the right company. If you don't love the profession of Relationship Marketing, what do you love about the products, services, people, mission, potential, or vision of your company? Find one aspect of it that you love or people you can connect with. If you cannot find one thing, then you'd better get out of it as quickly as possible so that you don't waste your time or anyone else's.

I do love this business — it embraces everything I need to feel of service, successful, and particularly fulfilled. Even though I never would have believed this at the get-go.

My sponsor Renee always says: *You have to bring who you are to what you do*, so if you like cutting hair — this is an excellent business for you.

If you like counselling — this is an excellent business for you.
If you like coaching — this is an excellent business for you.
If you like innovation — this is an excellent business for you.
If you like commerce — this is an excellent business for you.
If you like the service industry — this is an excellent business for you.
If you like health care — this is an excellent business for you.
If you like finance — this is an excellent business for you.
If you like beauty — this is an excellent business for you.
If you like decorating — this is an excellent business for you.
If you like writing — this is an excellent business for you.
If you like real estate — this is an excellent business for you.
If you like travel — this is an excellent business for you.
If you like teaching — this is an excellent business for you.
If you like computing — this is an excellent business for you.
If you like staying at home — this is an excellent business for you.
If you like art — this is an excellent business for you.
If you like self-development — this is an excellent business for

you.

If you like adventure — this is an excellent business for you.

If you like transformation — this is an excellent business for you.

It can practically wrap around any interest or profession. — How? — Because it has the potential to give you:

Greater health.
Time freedom.
Money freedom
An awesome community of people.
A networking group.
A personal development/leadership training program.
A sense of purpose and mission.
Your Tribe!

The important thing is not to limit who you think might be interested in achieving these benefits.

The common requirement is — you have to like people. The best Relationship Marketing companies are high-tech and high-touch — in other words you really do connect with the people you are working with. You have to resonate with the mission of the company.

It is a viable, credible, legitimate fair business being taught now in colleges and more and more professionals are getting on board. There's a good reason for this.

Like any new method or concept, it takes a while to be accepted by the masses but the pioneers who see the vision and take action, persevere, and never give up — pave the way and create the awareness in the world.

I truly am an ambassador for the profession and that is the polar opposite to my opinion when I was first presented with this business opportunity.

Now I want to stand on top of rooftops and shout:

Don't be afraid.

Come closer.

It is real.

It is profound.

It is brilliant.

And what rocks my world is, I get to witness beautiful transformation in people's lives, in their health, emotions, and relationships, and in their ability to have time and money freedom. And my Tribe is finding a way on a global scale.

I cannot believe my life today — I wake up in gratitude and I go to bed in gratitude — and what I love most of all, is that I have found the best mechanism for change and transformation I have ever witnessed. And you can, too.

Chapter 32

A Connecting Force

Flying out of Edmonton one day, looking out the window, I was pondering the whole idea: *Can I make a positive difference in the world?* (At 30,000 ft. there is very little interference.) After all, when I looked down below this vast expanse of universe, my perception was altered. Observing the flat squares for hundreds of miles below; sparsely spread farmhouses, and clusters of housing communities, I saw that they/I were just a dot on a dot on the screen; insignificant in size; miniscule in comparison. How on earth could I make a difference?

Then I thought about the people in the world who had made a big difference including: Jesus, Gandhi, Nelson Mandela, Warren Buffett, Oprah, and John Lennon, to name but a few. How had they made such a difference?

I suddenly got it. They are connectors of truth. They have created matrixes of communication, or perhaps in the case of Jesus, books (including the Bible) were written about his life, which have impacted the whole. Oprah is an icon in this area of communicating and telecasting out to the world. Bill Gates wanted a computer for everyone. Henry Ford wanted every household to own a car. How did they do this? They became the connecting force.

The emergence of technology, such as computers and different modes of transportation, connects us. What else connects us? Relationships connect us. When we communicate, we often come from such vastly different places that there is little ability to unite with the other...to find ways of connecting. Yet the relationship is the most important aspect of this process. The more we can meet people where they are at, the more rapport can happen. It's like learning to speak the same language.

Eckhart Tolle, once a humble hermit in the woods, is now exposed to the world through his books and message. I had the pleasure of spending the day with Eckhart at my Retreat Centre many years ago. I know he wanted to stay invisible but life had a different purpose for him. His work was needed for the arising consciousness of this planet and the mechanisms to share this appeared through Oprah. And we know what a catalyzing force she is.

I personally know a humble, billionaire philanthropist who wakes up every day and his only thought is: *How many people can I serve today?*

Somebody once told me that the degree to which a person connects to humanity in service– is usually the degree of abundance they can receive. It's like being a tower that receives for the many and disperses out from there. These people do this and they are abundant beyond compare. Philanthropic by nature, their desire is to serve mankind. These are the connectors.

I love that in Relationship Marketing we have the opportunity to connect through our hearts and service and become philanthropic contributors. When survival needs are met, we are much more able to help others. We can impact thousands of people and maybe more this way.

I was a reluctant leader at first. Then life picked me up through an accident and tossed me squarely into a profession where I could serve thousands and thousands of people. How clever...how graceful...how perfect. I am the connector of dreams and visions. I am a connector, a midwife, a coach and mentor. I am a mother and friend — leader and follower. I am the one who struggles and the one who excels. I love this mechanism of growth.

Suddenly my musing brought me back into the airplane.

I noticed the scene below morphed into giant-size, snow peaked mountains — The Rocky Mountains, with vast life forms and sparkling bodies of water glistening in between. Nothing came to mind here, just peacefulness arising and silence. No words came.

Appreciating the gorgeous blue infinity with pockets of wispy cotton clouds, I saw how one little dot on a dot of the screen could make a difference after all.

What you have to say and do matters. You are important and have a precious jewel to deliver. Do not waste this gift by keeping it locked away. The world needs your expression.

You are a unique, never to be repeated event, in the history of the Universe

–José Ortega y Gasset

About the Author

Angelyn Toth
Founder/Owner of Xenia Creative Development Centre on
Bowen Island, BC. Canada. www.xeniacentre.com

Since a child, Angelyn has been fascinated with the process of transformation, whether witnessing this in people or places. — It became her passion and life's work. Another big passion was and continues to be, horses and other animals.

Angelyn grew up in England and travelled to Canada in 1975 where she began working in a local radio station and later in the corporate world. This led her to her vocation in personal development where she was personally mentored by some great teachers, over many decades. She started her own business in 1986 where she focused on supporting people to grow and awaken to their greatest potential. Shortly thereafter Angelyn was blessed with a beautiful daughter who has been her greatest joy.

In 1994, Angelyn purchased a thirty-eight-acre, dilapidated old sheep farm to begin her vision of a sanctuary in nature where people could come to be inspired, revitalize their soul or be creative. Xenia Creative Development Centre was born and people started coming from all around the world. The transformation involved was a huge undertaking involving the support of hundreds of volunteers and hundreds of thousands of dollars.

A decade into the initiative, Angelyn underwent major financial stress and nearly lost her beloved Xenia back to the bank. At one point, she was five months behind in the mortgage, three years behind in property taxes and it was going in to the newspaper for a tax sale. She refers to this time of her life as her *dark night of the soul*. It lasted two long years. After surrendering to the terror she finally felt relief and started trusting her deeper inner guidance. Her life has been magical ever since she learned radical trust.

In 2005 Angelyn joined a Relationship Marketing company much to her surprise and in spite of her resistance. At first, she almost didn't recognize it as the miracle she had been praying for. And she wouldn't have but for the fortitude of a colleague who had visited her Retreat Centre many years earlier and strongly urged Angelyn to take a look at a business vehicle. A vision they both shared was to bring leaders from around the world together to have an impact on education, health and business. This was to be the vehicle to fulfill this vision.

Ten years later, Angelyn cannot believe the transformation in her own life and in the lives of those with whom she has worked. She has a wonderful team of loyal and dedicated people. Angelyn won the Associate of the Year Award for North America in 2008, for exemplary leadership and was inducted into the Millionaire Club, having personally earned one million dollars. She has served on the Field Advisory Board of her company for several years and is the top income earner in Canada. This year she was the recipient of the 2015 YunHo Lee Award. The most prestigious honor given by her company for servant leadership and dedication to purpose.

Having a successful Relationship Marketing business sustains her Retreat Centre, which is her labour of love and dedication. The biggest surprise of all was finding the perfect partnership and parallel path with her work of transformation. It fulfils her desire to serve others to awaken their greatest gifts and talents, while she enjoys the freedom to create, ride horses and write.

Connect with Angelyn via email: angelyntoth@gmail.com or visit her website: angelyntoth.com

About the Illustrator

Jessie Flynn

Jessie Flynn is a thirty-three-year-old artist whose preferred medium is Prismacolour pencil crayons and black ink. She enjoys creating pictures out of her imagination, as well as portraits of people and animals. She has recently illustrated a booked called *Hope* by Jackie Douglas and was in an art show in Kelowna B.C. She met Angelyn Toth when she was twenty-one and spent a lot of time at Xenia, Angelyn's beautiful, thirty-eight-acre Retreat Centre on Bowen Island. Angelyn saw Jessie's talent right away and over the years they felt inspired to do a project together. Xenia became a creative beacon and a home away from home for Jessie. She currently lives in Westbank B.C. with her fiancée Jessica, her German shepherd dogs and three cats. Her goals for the future involve getting her work on display in local coffee shops, enrolling in art shows, and possibly doing more projects with Angelyn Toth.

Angelyn is delighted to be showcasing Jessie's work in *From Squeak to Roar.*

To see or to buy more of Jessie's artwork go to:
http://www.facebook.com/jessieflynnpencilcrayonart

Printed in Canada